STARS
in the SKY

STORIES OF THE FIRST AFRICAN AMERICAN FLIGHT ATTENDANTS

CASEY GRANT

Wasteland Press

www.wastelandpress.net
Shelbyville, KY USA

Stars in the Sky:
Stories of the First African American Flight Attendants
by Casey Grant

Third Printing – November 2016
ISBN: 978-1-60047-545-0
Library of Congress Control Number: 2014955771

Thank heavens for my special friend and pre-publishing editor Susan Giffin. Because of your expertise and caring spirit, you made the last steps of getting my book ready for publication less stressful. Thanks for helping to make it happen.

—*Casey Grant*

Names have been changed to protect the privacy of some individuals
and their stories. I have tried to recreate some stories from memory,
research, and individual interviews. I apologize in advance for any
mistakes that might have entered the final text.

Printed in the U.S.A.

0   1   2   3   4   5   6   7   8   9   10   11   12

I would like to dedicate this book to my family. Thank you to my parents for having the courage to pursue your dreams and exposing my siblings and me to world travel. Thank you for showing love and supporting us in our own dreams. My sisters Jackie and Debbie are my best friends and support team. My favorite brother, Eric, not just because he is the only one we have but because I would have picked him as my brother if I had had the opportunity, and his wife, Janice. My perfect nieces, Barika and her husband Tony, Mia Cassandra (my namesake), Aniyah Grace, and my equally perfect nephews Grant, Gabriel, and Anton.

"There is no greater agony than bearing an untold story inside you."
Maya Angelou

AUTHOR'S NOTES

In all of the stories about aviation and its history, the stories of the first African American stewardesses have been left untold and unknown. We first took to the skies when flying was glamorous and exclusive, when little girls dreamt of being stewardesses, models, or movie stars. We rubbed elbows with the elite and traveled the world when few others could. We flew as pioneers in a global society long before the time of the Internet and globalization. We also kept our heads high, facing down racial prejudice and discrimination. We lived as stars of the sky. I was one of the first African American stewardesses for Delta Air Lines, and I worked alongside other pioneers for almost thirty-five years as co-adventurers and friends. This book tells my story and theirs.

Since *Stars in the Sky* came out in December 2014, I am pleased to say that it has won three prestigious awards: Here's to Life (by the singer Zemrah whose organization presents annual awards), NYCHA Branch of the NAACP's "Just R.E. A. D." Award, and the Bessie Coleman Aerospace Legacy, Inc. Award. In addition, I have received letters from President Barack H. Obama and Congressman John Lewis, acknowledging our contributions to the civil rights movement.

THANKS TO SPECIAL PEOPLE

I'd like to thank Hardie McKinney, my number one motivator and inspiration for writing my book, and other friends for encouraging me to write this story. Hardie made me realize the valuable significance of our place in the aviation world, and recognize the importance of our revealing and reliving the experiences we encountered while breaking through the barriers in the aviation world.

Of course the book couldn't have been written without the valuable input and support from my family: Jackie Hardmon, Eric and his wife Janice Grant, Debbie Sanchez, Pat and Barika Grant, Melinda Stapleton, Ralph Cox, Jerry Garcia, Janice and A.J. White, and Martha Kelly.

The "Delta Girls," or "fly girls," as we sometimes called ourselves: Patricia Grace Murphy, Phenola Culbreath Smith, Ann Thomas, Agatha Collins, Ruth Cooper, Sherry Austin, Elaine McKinney, Penny Boone, Sarah Qualls, Debbie Phillips, Debra Surrett, Terry Taylor, Bonnie Wall-Wilson, Verna Lott-Lewis, Loretta Mayes, Adelena Marshall, Gail Bibb, Flora Gant, Wanda Wilson, Rose Martel, Mae Wallace, Phyllis Calvin, Barbara Stennett, Deborah Holmes, Dot Daniels, Adrian Cooper, Davye Mable, Cynthia Gathings, Geri Walker, Pat Fontenot, Belinda Todd, Bobbie Anthony, Tanya Williams, Collie Johnson, Tina Meyers, Wanda Craft, Mary Ellen Walker-Harris, Carrian Rose, Cynthia White, Margaret Jamison, Shelly Crump, Carolyn Sykes, Gwen DeBlanc, DeeDee Reid, Toni Turner, Debbie Cherry, Jackie Freeman, Joyce Kearse, Carrian Rose, Gwen Hicks, Sharon Wright, Linda Lenox, Debbie Moore, JoAnn Horne, Debra Caldwell, Kim Boyce, Wendy Robinson, and Marion Beckett.

I'd also like to extend my thanks for the support and encouragement expressed over our many special lunch dates with Rahni Flowers, the owner of Van Clef Salon, who I consider to be the equivalent in talent to Vidal Sassoon in Chicago. He was also responsible for many of the "Stars in the Sky" glamorous hairstyles and cuts for many years as well as First Lady Michelle Obama's styles when she lived in the Windy City, and for the night of her first inaugural ball as First Lady.

A special "thank you" to my dear friend, John Bailey, one of our handsome pilots we were so proud of in the early years. Thanks for being only a phone call away when I needed some technical information.

Of course a special shout out to my special friends: Donna Nash, Tami Strawn, and Geraldine (Gerry) Trammell, Jerry Garcia, Vincent Wiggins, and Herbert Henderson for believing in me.

And a very special shout out to all my KickStarter pledgers that supported me in publishing my book: Jackie Hardmon, Eric and Janice Grant, Debbie Sanchez, Mia Sanchez, Pat Grant, Barika Grant, Wanda Wilson, Richmond and Judith Davis, William Lucy, A.J and Janice White, Geri Rogers, Debbie Phillips, Natalie Phillips, Donsanell Nash, Tamorah Strawn, Pat Wills, Ann Brown Robinson, Earl Holmes, Dr. Yvonne Wallace, Ann Feeney, Carla Salvo, Sharon Goss, Greg Archer, Charlotte Ford, Alus Green, John Wyatt, Lynette Smith, Debbie Kapnistos, Art Matthews, Nancy Heaton, Dr. D. Mosely, Dr. Joyce Hunter, Marta Prieto, Gail James, Phyllis Calvin, Barbara Stennett, Hardie and Elaine McKinney, Sarah Qualls, Flora Gant, Cynthia White, Gail Bibb, Kim Hysaw, Sharon Hirtzer, Juliette Norris, Nancy Voss, Sally Punch, Gwen Ross, Mary Ellen Walker Harris, Terry Taylor, Debra Surrett, Cathy Carroll, Bonnie Walls-Wilson, Patricia Fontenot, Dempres Sims, Satia Orange, Mae and Elizabeth Wallace, Kim Hysaw, Carrian Rose, Cheryl McDonald Dupree, John and Gerri Walker, Dot Daniels, Cynthia Gathings, Tina Christianson, JoAnne Henderson, Hiawatha Reeves, Pat and Rose Martel, Robert Khoe, Debra Taylor, Michael Rahni Flowers, Daryl Wells, Richard Forchion, Tyrone Haymore, Roxanne Connor, Elsa Hale, Denise Jones, Debbie Cherry, Gwen Ross, Blanche Swedberg, Jerry Garcia, Brittany, Mac and Jan Tatarsky, Patricia Johnson, and Kai Behnke.

A heartfelt acknowledgement goes out to Ann Feeney who has been the best friend and supporter any one could ask for and my dedicated editor for the duration of writing my book.

Thank you, Zemrah, for acknowledging the importance of the unknown and untold stories of pioneers in aviation. It was such a thrill to have been selected as one of the honorees at your "Here's To Life" concert. It was a night I will always remember.

If I have accidentally not mentioned you by name, I hope it will be a forgivable oversight. It took many loving prayers and well wishes from family and friends that walked with me to see my dream fulfilled. I love you all so very much.

TABLE OF CONTENTS

CHAPTER ONE: *How It All Started* 1

CHAPTER TWO: *Early History of Blacks in Aviation* 20

CHAPTER THREE: *Dreams Do Come True*.. 39

CHAPTER FOUR: *The Good, the Bad, the Unpleasant*........................... 48

CHAPTER FIVE: *May I Have Your Attention – The First Star Has Boarded*........ 53

CHAPTER SIX: *Coffee, Tea or –* 66

CHAPTER SEVEN: *A New Development*.. 84

CHAPTER EIGHT: *The People We Encountered* 92

CHAPTER NINE: *It's a New Day* 106

CHAPTER TEN: *Tragedies* 111

CHAPTER ELEVEN: *Going International* 116

CHAPTER TWELVE: *Giving Back*...123

CHAPTER THIRTEEN: *Frustrations in the Sky*..................................127

CHAPTER FOURTEEN: *Still We Rise*...141

I'VE LIVED

I've lived,

Not the life of champagne, caviar, fast cars or expensive clothes, but the life of the sights and sounds of the world

I've lived,

I've seen the pyramids, crossed the Nile, and marveled at the sight of the Sphinx

Listened to the sounds of Bob Marley and seen Paris from the top of the Eiffel Tower

I've lived,

Witnessed my daughter's journey into adulthood, read Wright, Baldwin and Hughes

Fallen in and out of love and gotten chills when singing *Lift Every Voice and Sing*

I know there is much more to life, but if I never experience another sunrise or sunset, I have no regrets about the life I've lived

Eric B. Grant

CHAPTER ONE:

How It All Started

"I reflect the things I am and
anticipate the things I am to become."
Casey Grant

MAYBE IT WAS DESTINY that I spend nearly thirty-five years of my life flying around in a long metal tube, up to thirty thousand feet above sea level. I was born at Eglin Air Force Base in Florida and was raised in a small military town in Rantoul, Illinois, about fifteen miles from Champaign, home of the University of Illinois. In 1960, because of the Chanute Air Force Base, the population was around twenty-seven thousand, and the base was the biggest employer in town. Residents worked as clerks, photographers, cleaning staff, and in many other roles at the base. When the base closed in 1993, it hit the town hard and the population declined to fourteen thousand by 2010.

The base itself was a part of black aviation history. In 1941 the famous first all-black combat unit, the 99th Pursuit Squadron (later renamed the 99th Fighter Squadron), was created. The pilots trained at Tuskegee, while the ground crews trained at Chanute Army Air Field (as it was called then) from 1941 through 1943. These elite pilots, later known as the Tuskegee Airmen for their training or "Red Tails" for the red-painted tails on their Mustang planes, flew escort for heavy bomber missions in the heart of Germany.

During their missions, not a single bomber was lost to enemy fire, thanks not only to the skill and courage of the pilots, led by Colonel Benjamin O. Davis, Jr., but also to the effectiveness of the ground crews. One of these Tuskegee Airmen, James H. Harvey III, won the inaugural Top Gun Award in 1949, but the air force did not publicly credit him until fifty-four years later. In an article, which appeared in the *Deseret News* on February 12, 2012, author Steve Fidel states, "Fighter pilot with Tuskegee Airmen said impossible conditions sharpened black flying crews."

∽o∾

ILLINOIS AND THE CHICAGO-LAND AREA were home to many firsts and other accomplishments in black aviation. Cornelius Coffey was an extremely talented mechanical engineer who worked for Emil Mack, a local Chevrolet dealer, with another black engineer, John C. Robinson. In 1929 they both applied to and were accepted to the Curtiss-Wright School of Aeronautics in Chicago. When they showed up to attend classes, their admission was revoked because of their race. Mack, a white man, sued the school on their behalf.

During the day, Robinson worked as a janitor at the school. He saw an ad in a discarded magazine for the only airplane that could be constructed at home, the Heath Parasol airplane, an American single-seat open cockpit plane. Robinson and Coffey successfully assembled the plane but were not trained to fly it. One of the Curtiss-Wright instructors inspected the plane and was so impressed that he took it on a test flight. The instructor later spoke on behalf of Robinson and

Coffey that the school should admit them to private night classes because of their race.

They finished the program in 1931, Coffey graduating first in his class and Robinson graduating second. They so successfully demonstrated that blacks could be excellent pilots that the school actually invited them to return and teach classes to African American students. Robinson and Coffey became the first black instructors to teach at the first accredited flight school in the Midwest to admit America's pioneering black pilots.

Only one local airport, Akers, allowed them to use its facilities, and when Akers closed down, Robinson and Coffey, along with several students and other pilots, established the Challenger Aero Club (named for the Curtiss Challenger Engine).

In 1930 the club bought land south of Chicago, in Robbins, Illinois, which was one of Chicago's first suburbs with a predominantly black population, and built the airstrip with their own hands. This Robbins Airport was the first black-owned and operated airport in the nation. Janet Harmon, the only female in the class and the first black female commercial pilot, purchased an airplane for the club's use. Several local communities opposed the creation of the airstrip, and sometimes police from those communities came into Robbins to arrest the black pilots. At the Robbins History Museum, Tyrone Haymore, the director and curator, has a fascinating collection of artifacts from that era.

In 1933 a violent storm destroyed the entire facility. Fred and William Schumacher, the two brothers who owned the local Harlem Airport, invited the club to use their airport. The Harlem Airport was segregated, with two hangars for the white pilots and two for the blacks, although both used the airstrips.

Willa Beatrice Brown joined the club and became the first black woman to earn a private pilot's license in the United States. She also asked *The Chicago Defender* to help promote the club and flying to black audiences. In 1938 she and Coffey established the Coffey School of Aeronautics.

As World War II loomed, Coffey, Brown, and others decided to expand their efforts and form the National Airmen's Association. They did not want black pilots to be excluded from the ongoing efforts to train civilians as pilots and so decided on a publicity stunt to show off their capabilities.

Two members flew to Washington DC, making several landings to promote the cause. There they met Harry S. Truman, then only a senator. He was so impressed that he promised to promote their cause, and, in 1939 the airports selected as training sites for civilian pilots included seven black students, including Tuskegee. Further, some scholars believe that President Truman's order to integrate the armed services in 1948 was at least partially motivated by their flights.

John C. Robinson, Coffey's first collaborator, enlisted in the Ethiopian Air Force in WWII as a supreme commander to help defend it from Italian occupation, so he was one of the very first black aviation combat heroes.

∾o∿

MY OWN FATHER, ERIC GRANT, volunteered for the army in his early twenties and was stationed in New Guinea during World War II. Fighting in the lush tropical jungle during his tour of duty, he contracted malaria, which, in the Pacific killed or disabled almost as many troops as the enemy did. He lost his eyesight (probably due to the quinine used to treat malaria) near the end of his duty. He returned to the United States, unsure if his sight would ever return, but it did almost six months later, presumably when the last of the quinine left his system.

When he finished his tour of duty two years later and returned to the job force, he wasn't able to find employment in a segregated America, where separate drinking fountains and bathrooms were still the practice. To be the provider he wanted to be, he returned to the military in 1948, this time enlisting in the air force. The service still wasn't fully integrated then; blacks lived on one side of the base and whites on the other. In January of that same year, President Harry Truman ended segregated services, but some bases, like Eglin Field Air Force Base, still had segregated quarters. Blacks and whites had separate living quarters and even the playgrounds were segregated.

Our parents knew that my father's name, which didn't give any indication of his ancestry, had helped his career. He could apply for positions with his documented record and be awarded promotions. At times, he'd go for an interview, and somebody would come out into the waiting room and call out, "Eric Grant." He'd stand up and the official would respond, "No, Eric Grant." "I'm Eric Grant." Once he had his foot in the door like that, his record and professional demeanor spoke for themselves, and he was promoted steadily, faster than he might have been in a civilian career. Because of this, our parents made sure to give us names that could fit any ethnicity— Jacqueline, Eric, Emelda, and Deborah.

Mother wanted to be a nurse but got married instead when she fell in love with handsome Eric Grant. Being a nurse was truly her dream, and when he made it clear that if they were to be married, he wanted his family with him. He couldn't abide the idea of being a remote father and husband, and she didn't want this for her marriage and family either, so she gave up this dream for another one—a family. I think my father provided a good life for my mother, giving her a safe home life, security, and love. He always showed his appreciation for all she did to give their family a wonderful home, and she never second-guessed her decision to become a homemaker rather than a nurse.

My mother had a great sense of design and was a true homemaker—I'd have backed her in a decorating and interior design style against B. (Barbara) Smith or Martha Stewart any day. She was also incredibly thrifty and found ways to decorate like a queen on a small budget. For example, my father worked in the supply department, and sometimes when there was surplus material or other items that couldn't be used, he'd bring them home. She would look through designs from catalogs and magazines and anything else that caught her eye for style. Once she transformed surplus parachute material into bedspreads and curtains. It wasn't uncommon for us to leave one morning for school from bedrooms decorated in yellow and to return that afternoon to find that mother had transformed the old chenille bedspreads, dyed the parachute material lavender, and added a fringe.

Mother was also an inventive cook and displayed the same flair for cooking that she did for decoration. She could take any recipe from her books or magazines and adapt it to make it healthier, more affordable, or just plain better. One dinner, we were having what I thought was golden-brown fried chicken, and I couldn't understand why nobody else was eating as enthusiastically as usual. I wasn't going to let this opportunity slide, and each time I asked for another piece, she said, "Sure, help yourself."

After dinner, she put the leftover pieces in a bowl on the counter, and I ran out to play in the remaining daylight. However, my mind was still on that delicious food. I excused myself from my friends several times to return to the kitchen and ask for another piece. I didn't find out until later that the reason the rest of the family hadn't been chowing down like I had was that they weren't chicken legs; they were frog legs. Oh, well, at least I can truly say, "Tastes like chicken to me." (I'll also admit that in our family, I was the one who had a hearty appetite, to put it the polite way, or just plain greedy, to be less polite. No points for guessing which way my brother and sister put it.)

Our father finished high school in the services. He was proud of this accomplishment and made certain to seize all the opportunities available to him. He was personable, good-looking, and always made certain that he was well-groomed—the image of a capable and ambitious young military man. His duties included distributing supplies such as guns, helmets canteens, shoes, and uniforms to the enlisted, what today we'd call supply chain management. His intellect, determination, and personality led to steady promotions during his military career. He was so well suited for it and enjoyed the opportunities it gave him, as well as the chances that it gave him to serve his country. He retired from the air force with the rank of senior master sergeant in 1963.

He and my mother were proud of us and wanted us to represent ourselves, our family, and our race with all possible determination, skill, and drive. We looked up to them and to other people as we grew up. My aunt Nicky (who wasn't actually an aunt but my mother's best friend) was married to a lieutenant colonel in the air force, and, like my mother, somebody who was refined and ladylike without being at all artificial. She had a certain air of command around her, of somebody who expected to be listened to when she spoke. I admired her not only for her demeanor but also for her education and her beautiful way of speaking. She was a teacher, and when I understood that she wasn't just smart but highly educated, this fired my own ambition to become educated. I thought of her when I fulfilled this ambition years later.

My mother's first cousin, Alice Coachman-Davis, was my hero growing up, and every time she was featured in *Ebony*, we were so proud for her. My mother would always share stories about her and how they grew up together in Georgia. Alice was a track and field athlete, the first African American female to win a gold medal in the high jump in the 1948 London Summer Olympics. Not only was she the first black woman and thus first African American female to win a gold medal, she was also the only American woman to win a gold medal that year. Alice had to overcome not only the obstacles of racism but also of her family's first opposition to her practicing sports. But she didn't back down. Of course, I also looked up to the leaders of the Civil Rights movement, but I was fortunate to have so many close role models of women who showed leadership, determination, and grace.

Armed with stories like hers and their high expectations, our parents drove us to achieve the best that we could and to stand up for ourselves. When my brother was six, he and some of his friends accidentally strayed onto the white children's playground. The white children immediately started calling them names and trying to chase them off. My brother and his friends briefly decided to stay and fight but then retreated before either side could get physically hurt, although the name calling certainly hurt their feelings.

Our home was open to all of the young military men who were lonely and homesick. Our father believed in family and extended family, and he made sure that they could come in and immediately feel embraced and under his good influence. On some holidays, many of these young men spent their Christmas with us, and there was always a present under the tree for every single person.

✂∘✄

WHEN MY FATHER WAS POSTED TO A BASE IN ENGLAND, my mother took us by ship to join him (when ships were more common than planes for crossing the Atlantic). We were the only black family on the ship to England and many of the other travelers had never seen a black family before. Our parents taught us to be respectful to everybody we met, and we were in fact so well-behaved that many people congratulated our mother on our behavior.

After that long trip, we lived in South Cherney, a little town just off the base, and I went to a local school. Of our three years there, I vividly remember the little, two-story, brown brick house with the narrow cobblestone walkway that led to the courtyard where my neighborhood friends and I played kickball or rode our tricycles. The houses weren't equipped with central heating, so we had to put a small gas heater in each room. Taking a hot bath took a little more preparation than just putting in the stopper and turning the hot water handle. Instead we had to heat the water at the stove, carry it to the tub, and then add it to the cold tap water. We also had what the British called a "honeydew bucket," which sounds a lot nicer than it was. It was what the houses had before flush toilets, and my father had the undesirable weekly chore of taking it to the communal waste disposal. That was what all the fathers in the village did every Sunday night, rain or shine. When people get nostalgic for the good old English traditions, I think that's not one that comes to their minds.

At first we felt like foreigners, but I was soon comfortable with the local British dialect, learning to call mother "Mum" and being instructed by the "bobbies" (local term for policemen) on how to cross the street and ride tricycles. In the school gym, we were instructed to stand in the lines on the floor, and when the bobby blew his whistle and raised his hand, we stopped or proceeded when he waved us to pass or cross the intersection.

I was too little to understand what it all meant, but all of England was thrilled by the June coronation of Elizabeth II, the oldest daughter of King George VI. When he had become too ill to travel, she was crowned queen. While the event itself was on June 2, 1953, that entire summer was full of celebrations and ceremonies. London was packed with throngs to see the coronation and even more people were glued to their televisions to watch. This was actually a minor controversy: Several members of the government, including the Archbishop of Canterbury and Winston Churchill, expressed their reservations about whether this was "right and proper" and whether Elizabeth would be able to withstand the additional strain of the heat and glare from the cameras. The soon-to-be queen insisted that nothing would prevent "her people being able to participate."

A few weeks earlier, the headmaster of my brother's school called him into his office, and my brother automatically assumed that he was in trouble. (It wasn't exactly the first time he'd been called in. Or the second. Or, let's face it, the tenth.) Instead, the headmaster handed him a letter to take home and give to my parents, with assurance that (this time) it wasn't a report on his behavior.

Instead, he had been chosen to be a part of the ceremony at Oxford College, where some of his schoolmates were to put on a play to celebrate the coronation. Princess Margaret, the queen's younger sister, was the guest of honor, and Eric was selected to give her a specially bound copy of the script. At the conclusion of the play, carrying the script on a satin pillow, he approached her, knelt with a flourish that he had practiced all week, and presented it to her. My parents were very proud Americans but didn't mind his serving English royalty, just this one time.

WHEN I WAS ABOUT SEVEN, WE LEFT FOR CALIFORNIA—Castle Air Force Base in Fresno. Once again we felt like foreigners because now we had to call our mother "Mom" instead of "Mum" and remember that father wasn't driving on the wrong side of the road. Of course in those days without cable and the Internet, we didn't know the cartoons or cowboy shows that were familiar to our new classmates. My older brother and sister's friends were astonished that we didn't even know about *I Love Lucy* or *The Three Stooges*. This was uncomfortable at first, unlike flush toilets, which we welcomed back into our lives very eagerly.

We stayed in California two years, long enough for America and California to feel deeply familiar. Then my father came home one day and said that we'd be stationed in Africa. Through the eyes of an eight-year-old, this was going to be a jungle adventure with lions and tigers and bears (as Dorothy in the *Wizard of Oz* said), and I was excited and scared by the prospect. My sister, brother, and I had seen Tarzan at the movies often enough to be sure that we knew exactly what it would be like, and so did our classmates, who were vicariously thrilled at the thought. Fine for them—they didn't have to wonder if they'd be eaten by lions!

STARTING IN 1957, WE WERE STATIONED IN TRIPOLI, LIBYA, in North Africa, which is closer to Egypt than to the sub-Saharan jungle we had imagined. We saw Arabs dressed in traditional clothing—men wearing long robes over baggy pants, and women wearing the burqa, which covered them from head to toe, with only the eyes showing, making me wonder how they could even see. They were accompanied by their flocks of animals, looking almost as though nothing had changed since Biblical times. For us, it was a thrill but also profoundly disorienting to be sharing the road with sheep and camels. We got used to camels spitting on the car any time we drove by them, and otherwise showing their profound disdain for humans.

Even then, there was tension, and Americans, especially ones affiliated with the military, weren't welcome or warmly received. Muammar Gaddafi was then a young, self-described "simple revolutionary," fighting for, among other things, an end to the American presence in Libya. In 1969 a few years after we left, he led a successful coup and became the absolute ruler of Libya. (He himself was overthrown and killed in a revolution in 2011.) The service men were continually warned about the dangers of frequenting certain areas downtown. Still, some airmen disappeared and were later found dead, or never found at all.

Our parents, however, shielded us from more than a very vague knowledge of these dangers so we weren't afraid of the people. In fact, we encountered the legendary Middle East hospitality, and people would offer us tea with peanuts or other treats. Friday was market day, and I remember all the hustle and bustle in the streets. I especially remember watching from the school bus window as animals were led to the slaughterhouse, where, according to Islamic halal practices, they were drained of all their blood. The floors ended up covered in blood from all the slaughtered sheep, camels, chickens, and other animals, so much so that the slaughterhouse workers were up to their ankles. While of course I knew then that meat comes from living animals and doesn't just appear in the supermarket in neat packages, it was a shock to see all of that. Perhaps it was another sign that I was born for a life of switching from place to place and culture to culture, since although I thought all the blood was gross and it left a very vivid impression, it didn't make me any less curious or inclined to explore.

We arrived in Libya during Ramadan, the ninth month of the Islamic lunar calendar. During Ramadan, observant Muslims abstain from eating, drinking, smoking, and sexual intercourse from sunup to sundown. At sundown, Muslims have the Iftar, a traditional meal that begins with eating dates, in honor of Mohammed's practice.

All Muslims are obligated to pray five times a day, and this is especially important during Ramadan. Imams (the equivalent to priests or pastors) sound the call to prayer from the minarets of their mosques in a traditional chant that is based on Middle Eastern tonalities. To our ears, this sounded very strange, since we were familiar with only the European scale and tonalities. During this time, the military impressed on us that we had to be respectful during this holy period. For kids our age, not being able to mimic the sounds we heard during the calls to prayer felt unfair, but the military and our parents were firm on this matter.

Because the official sundown time was so important, it was announced each night with the sound of cannon. This always startled us even though we knew what it was for and knew it was coming. Other sounds overwhelmed us, too. Anybody complaining about a loud car alarm on the street outside should listen to a donkey braying—all night long.

As for the sights, it was our first exposure to true poverty. Living on military bases or in a small village in England wasn't rubbing shoulders with the rich and richer, but the families were all roughly middle class. Some were better off, some were worse off, but nobody we saw lived in abject poverty. This all changed in Libya.

When we saw kids our age clearly without the nice things that we had or the nice home we lived in, this hit us hard. We regularly saw young children standing on the sides of the roads as we slowly drove by, begging for food or money with their hands out, sometimes all day. I remember looking at their innocent faces and seeing flies crawling in and around their eyes and mouths. The children never seemed to be annoyed or swat them away. Nevertheless, I instinctively swatted at my own face to suggest that they do the same, as I might do to catch somebody's eye, or wipe my mouth to signal someone to remove food stuck there.

We lived through the middle of the Suez Canal crisis, which started in October 1956. After the Egyptians nationalized the Suez Canal, the British and French governments arranged for Israel to attack Egypt and to use the ensuing conflict to ensure that the Canal would remain available for Western oil interests.

We directly witnessed the protests against the British, French, and Americans who worked for different oil companies and lived across the street from us. This was the first time I had ever seen such a protest. People chanted, screamed, and waved signs, raging against the oil companies and Western governments. Every day, we would stand on our balcony and watch them protest and picket the families. We couldn't understand exactly what they were saying, but their anger was evident. This went on for a few weeks, and my father told us the base had been placed on high alert, which meant that my father and the other military personnel were allowed to travel only back and forth to work and to be prepared to be recalled to the base at any time. The military put us on lockdown at our house. This gave us time for some family bonding, playing games, and acting like children.

We moved once there was housing on base. This saved my father from having to drive to the base every day, which took thirty to forty-five minutes, depending on weather, the roads, traffic, and of course camels. Camels don't believe in moving out of the way for anybody or anything, and if one decided to walk slowly in front of a car, the driver just had to wait.

After we moved to the base, two new classmates, both African American, and I soon became friends. Donna Dickey from California and Jean Abram from New Orleans also had fathers working on the base. Our families soon met and bonded in the way that is typical in nearly any country, where people from the same country who speak the same language will gravitate toward one another. We're still friends to this day.

I was now adjusting to school, new friends, and new culture, customs, and country. I didn't realize that another upheaval was on its way. Our parents had kept a very important secret from us children: there was to be a new arrival to the Grant family in about seven months. I was the last to be told because I was the youngest in the family, the most tenderhearted emotionally, and I was going to have to relinquish my role as the baby of the family.

That news shattered me to the point that my grades suffered, and I became very withdrawn in school, a marked change from my normal tendency of being talkative to the point occasionally of being disruptive. When my parents realized what was happening, my father reassured me that I would still be "his baby girl." So on November 21, 1957, Debbie made her entrance. My sister Jackie and I loved this pretty, little, curly-haired baby sister (and toy!), and she was soon a big focus in our lives. Even though she has become a very accomplished educator in the Chicago Public School system, she is still our baby sister.

∽o∽

I WAS ABOUT TEN WHEN WE CAME BACK TO THE UNITED STATES in 1960 to Chanute Air Force Base in Rantoul, Illinois. We felt like foreigners all over again in farm town, Illinois. For us as schoolchildren, this meant that even though we had far more life experience than our classmates, we were several years behind in fashion, knowing the latest songs, and being familiar with the latest television shows, like *American Bandstand, Amos and Andy,* and other popular shows. (Remember, kids, this was all before multiple television sets in the household. We watched what our parents watched.) The transition was easier than it might sound; we always had the support of our family, knew about travel and adjustments, and had the natural resilience and adaptability of children, so we settled in easily. While I didn't know much about television shows, I did know hopscotch, and I met Janice Davis-White while playing that game. Later I met Loretta Martin, who would also become a good friend, since our fathers worked together.

As a kid, I first wanted to be a nurse, just like so many girls my age. We all wanted to be good nurturers, taking care of people and making them feel better. However, the thought of seeing the world was still in the back of my mind, and so when I entered high school, I thought that upon graduation, I'd join the navy. I knew I wanted to travel the world, experience different cultures and customs, and meet new people.

Sandy Golden, a high school girlfriend who was a year older, went into the army. During her basic training, she called me up and told me not even to think about joining the military. Her details about the difficult training and getting up every morning at the crack of dawn made a deep first impression. That convinced me that I had to see the world some other way. Nobody was there to tell me that stewardesses get up at the crack of dawn and often earlier. I hadn't escaped that fate.

My very first job out of high school was at the cafeteria on base. I also took night classes in business skills from the University of Illinois at Champaign/ Urbana, which was about twenty-five minutes away.

My next job was much more intense. Maybe it was my mother's influence, but photography and the visual aspect of things always appealed to me, so I got a job at the Chanute Photography Studio, first in sales and then, working my way up, head photographer and lead sales person. In fact, the company asked me to open a new branch in St. Louis, but that wasn't enough incentive to make me leave my family. The Vietnam War was still raging and the Chanute Photography Studio was the only professional studio on base. We photographed the military graduating classes and also took photographs in the studio for these young men to send to their families or sweethearts. I could never escape the realization that for those headed to Vietnam, this might be the last photograph that their families and loved ones might have.

My sister Jackie was working for the university for the Clerical Learning Program, which trained high school girls for jobs by teaching typing and other clerical work, and they also sent us out on job interviews. I still hadn't decided exactly what I wanted, so I applied for the program. After completing it, I successfully interviewed for a job in the office of the president of the university, working for the president's secretary, Frances G. Dickman.

She and I became very close after just a short time on the job. Frances married late in life and didn't have any children. As soon as we bonded, she virtually adopted me as a daughter and our families soon became close as well.

One time, Fran and I were talking about how a friend of hers was going to take a management position with Delta. We had often talked about how much I wanted a career that would let me see the world, and that sparked an idea in her head, so she mentioned me to him. He told her that, next time he was in town, he'd like to meet me as an informal interview for a stewardess position.

Like the rest of the world, I thought that for those chosen to become stewardesses, the world suddenly opened up into something made out of pure glamour. I knew that if I made it into that select group, the world would be mine.

While stewardesses were glamorous, they also had a very ladylike, even pristine aura about them. I later discovered that the truth—and some passengers' perceptions—were different, but then, that ladylike image, perched high on her pedestal, fit with my dreams as well. My older sister, Jackie, still my confidante and the first person I go to for advice, had given my girlfriends and me a talk about the birds and bees. She had totally convinced us that experimenting with sex was something we should wait to do until we were older and married. We thought Jackie was wise and would never lead us astray, so if she thought this was what we should do, it was good enough for us. We had also listened to some of our classmates talk about the exact consequences of moonlit nights in the cornfields, including new members of the family that appeared nine months later.

During my first job interview, I talked about my travel experiences and previous jobs, including some modeling at fashion shows for local department stores such as the local branch of Carson Pirie Scott, my continuing education, and my progressive responsibility at the Chanute Photography Studio. After lunch, Barry told me to give Fran my two-week notice and to send in a formal application to Delta, just to have everything officially on file. He had hired me to be a stewardess. Fran was delighted with the news. In fact, she insisted on being the one who typed my official application for stewardess training and sent it off. I was on my way.

CHAPTER TWO:

Early History of Blacks in Aviation

B EFORE I GO FURTHER WITH MY STORY, I'd like to set the scene and pay tribute to the first black flight attendants and pilots. One of the first women to inspire us was a pilot, Bessie Coleman, who died tragically early in 1926. Only a few years after her death, she briefly lapsed into obscurity; few outside the aviation world or who remembered milestones of black history knew her name. Since then, though, the United States honored her with U.S. Postal Service stamp, and many locations near airports are named in her honor, not only in the United States but internationally. In Chicago in 1990, the city renamed a major road (Old Mannheim Road) Bessie Coleman Drive.

Bessie Coleman once said, "The air is the only place free from prejudices." Born in Atlanta, Texas, on January 26, 1892, she was the tenth of thirteen children born to a poor sharecropper family. While she showed an early talent for math, she had to drop out of college due to a lack of funds. She worked as a manicurist in Chicago and heard stories of the World War I pilots. Those stories made her dream of being a pilot herself, but no flight school in the United States would admit a black woman.

Two other pioneers heard of her and decided she deserved to follow this dream. They were Robert S. Abbott, the founder and publisher of *The Chicago Defender*, and Jesse Binga, founder of Binga State Bank. *The Chicago Defender* was one of the most influential newspapers of its time in the black community. It unrelentingly documented racial disparities and lynchings in the South and featured the stories of blacks who had successfully migrated to the North, finding better employment opportunities and less discrimination. Some historians even credit it for driving the Great Migration, when approximately 1.6 million African Americans moved from the rural South to the urban North between 1910 and 1930, and another 5 million migrated between 1940 and 1970.

Jesse Binga moved from Detroit to found a bank that would serve blacks in Chicago, something that many white-owned banks refused to do. Then, as now, access to banking could mean the difference between financial success and struggling, if only as a safe place to put money where it couldn't be stolen. While there were formal and informal mutual help groups for blacks, banks also were a vital source of loans for education, a home, or to start a business.

Mr. Abbott and Mr. Binga encouraged Ms. Coleman to go to Paris and study aviation. Back then, Paris was far freer from prejudice than the United States, and so she sailed there on November 20, 1920. After she finished her studies, she received her license from the Federation Aeronautique Internationale and became the first black woman in the world to have an international pilot's license.

She returned to the United States in 1921 and became a media sensation. The public called her Queen Bess; she was one of the most famous barnstormers—stunt pilots—in the country. Audiences were happy to pay to watch her perform at places such as the Checkerboard Airdrome, now known as Chicago's Midway Airport. There, she performed daredevil stunts like loops, figure eights, and exhilarating near-ground dips. She risked her life each time, but Queen Bess actually died in a far more mundane way.

She was in her own new Curtis JN-4 aircraft, which she had planned to fly in an air show the next day in Jacksonville, Florida. William Wills, her mechanic and publicity agent, was the pilot. She was in the other seat, looking over the cockpit sill to view the terrain and figure out the logistics for a parachute jump, so she wasn't in her seatbelt. Ten minutes after takeoff, the plane failed to recover from a dive and spun out of control. Ms. Coleman was thrown from the aircraft and fell to her death.

Further investigation revealed that a wrench, which had been used to service the engine the day before, had carelessly been left in the engine. During the flight, it slid forward and wedged in the gearbox, which caused the aircraft to spin out of control.

Like many celebrities, Ms. Coleman was forgotten soon after her death. She had planned a lasting monument and resource for other African Americans who dreamed of flying, a flight school that would admit all races, but died before she could fulfill this second dream of hers. Those of us who dreamed about careers in aviation did not forget. Even so, it was almost twenty years after her death that the skies opened for more than a few of us.

∽๑∾

WHILE WE THINK OF THE 1950S AND 1960S AS THE CIVIL RIGHTS ERA, it started earlier than that. In 1944, the New York State Committee against Discrimination proposed legislation to create a permanent commission that would enforce equal rights and opportunities for employment. On March 12, 1945, New York Governor Thomas E. Dewey signed in to law the Ives-Quinn Anti-Discrimination Bill. New York thus became the first state to make it illegal to discriminate against anyone on the basis of race, religion, or creed. There had been other legislation before, but this was the most comprehensive and powerful. When it didn't create the economic disaster for the state that its opponents had declared it would make inevitable, other states followed suit, though there was still no national legislation.

The first Negro (the preferred term then) stewardess was Patricia Banks. She completed stewardess training at Grace Downs Air Career School in 1956 and attended interviews with airlines but became confused when her classmates got hired and she didn't. Finally, her head stewardess told Ms. Banks she wasn't getting hired because the airlines did not employ blacks.

Realizing she was a victim of race discrimination, and with the encouragement of Representative Adam Clayton Powell, she filed a complaint against TWA, Mohawk, and Capital Airlines. Before her case was brought to court, the statute of limitations had expired on her complaints against TWA and Mohawk, but her case was allowed to move forward against Capital Airlines.

Eventually, the courts ordered Capital Airlines to hire Ms. Banks, but in December, 1957, Mohawk Airlines, a regional carrier, hired the first Negro stewardess, Ruth Carol Taylor, so she was technically the first one to take to the air. Her inaugural flight was on February 11, 1958, from Ithaca, New York, to New York City.

Taylor flew for Mohawk Airlines only for six months before she married. Then it was common practice for stewardesses (and other working women, such as teachers) to be dismissed once they married. A few were allowed to keep working as married women but had to quit if they became pregnant.

Also during 1958, TWA hired their first black stewardess, Margaret Grant, out of eight hundred applicants. Unfortunately, her training was cut short when she was diagnosed with sickle cell anemia. This condition, in which red blood cells, instead of being round and soft, are curved and hardened, is particularly common among blacks. Living or even flying at high altitudes can stress the spleen and increase the risk of complications for sickle cell anemia, so she had to leave the program.

$$\sim 0 \infty$$

BLACKS WERE ALSO ENTERING THE COCKPIT AS PILOTS. Marlon Green joined the United States Air Force, where his last posting was flying the SA-16 Albatross with the 36th Air Rescue Squadron at Johnson Air Base in Tokyo, Japan. He also had flown B-25s during WWII. While on leave, he read a newspaper article stating that several United States airlines had started hiring regardless of race.

Green applied for several jobs but never heard back. He finally filled out the application form for Continental, leaving the question about race unanswered and not attaching a picture. Continental invited him to interview, but, despite his having more flight hours than any of the white applicants, he was rejected.

He filed a legal complaint, and the local anti-discrimination commission found that the airline had denied him solely because of his race, which was illegal in the state of Colorado, Continental's base. It still refused to employ him until 1963, when the case made it to the United States Supreme Court, which ruled in Mr. Green's favor. Mr. Green then became the first African American pilot for Continental Airlines. However, while Marlon Green's case was still being heard,

American Airlines hired Dave Harris in 1965, making him the first commercial black airline pilot. (Shades of Patricia Banks Edmiston) Fifty years later, Continental named one of their new Boeings, a 737, in Marlon Green's honor.

On September 24, 1966, President Lyndon B. Johnson implemented a federal order for affirmative action, making it illegal for organizations to discriminate against religious, ethnic, or racial minorities, and opening many more opportunities for people of all backgrounds.

Four months earlier, Delta Air Lines hired their first African American stewardess, a gracious, pretty, twenty-one-year-old lady from Chicago: Patricia Grace Murphy. Whether the world was ready or not, Patricia arrived on the scene and broke the barrier for us on Delta. In 1968 Delta changed its slogan to "Delta is ready when you are," and we joked that Patricia had helped make Delta ready. In 1967 Delta hired their first African American pilots: Sam Graddy, John Qualls, Fred Boone, and John Bailey, and they were followed by many more. We were filled with pride each time we saw one of our handsome pilots walk down the concourse, wearing their uniforms with those gleaming stripes and big gold wings pinned on the chests of their jackets. Everything about them screamed, "I'm in command," and we felt like they represented us as well.

When I interviewed Patricia almost forty years later, I asked her what it was like to have been the first. She said in her usual composed and soft-spoken manner that the company had been very protective of her from the beginning. After graduation, a supervisor, June Heuerman, told her that there were only two bases where they could send her: New Orleans or Chicago. When she asked why, they explained that those were the only locations that they thought she'd be able to find housing close to the airport. She had grown up in Chicago and was going to be based there, so she was surprised when her supervisor urged her to look for a few particular apartments because they "would rent to you." Patricia didn't understand what that meant, never having tried to rent an apartment in a neighborhood where blacks weren't welcome.

∽o∾

DURING THOSE TIMES, IT WAS EQUALLY DIFFICULT FOR AFRICAN AMERICANS to find hotels when they were traveling. Between 1936 and 1966, during the Jim Crow era of enforced segregation, blacks were regularly refused service at hotels, gas stations, and restaurants, especially in the South. This created a market niche for a new publication, *The Negro Motorist Green Book*. Victor H. Green, a U.S postal worker and travel agent, created this guide not only to provide a list of hotels, gas stations, and restaurants that would serve blacks, but also to warn travelers about "sundown towns," places where blacks had to be outside the town limits by nightfall.

One black author, John A. Williams, in his 1965 book, *This Is My Country Too*, wrote that white travelers could not imagine what an African American experienced in traveling, that they have no "idea of how much nerve and courage it required for a Negro to drive coast to coast in America." He even advised any black man driving his own car in the South to wear a chauffeur's cap, so that nobody would react aggressively.

The last issue appeared before Delta hired Patricia Grace Murphy. However, the attitudes that made it necessary didn't disappear along with the publication, and as Patricia and several others of us found out, even in cities large enough to have airports, hotels and apartments could be hostile environments.

She started her apartment search with buildings that weren't on the list Delta gave her, and after several rejections, she realized that she'd better go back to June Heuerman and ask for help. The base manager immediately asked two white stewardesses, who had just found an apartment, if they'd be willing to share with her. They immediately welcomed her warmly as their roommate. Later, she was able to find her own apartment near the airport where there were already a number of stewardesses. We called these stewardess communities "Stew Zoos," and nearly every major city, or at least the ones where an airline has a base, boasts one or more.

Patricia's first few trips were exciting, not just because of the new life and travel, but because she saw firsthand how her colleagues reacted to Delta's first black stewardess. Being a trailblazer like this gave her a thrill but also a tremendous sense of responsibility. The training and requirements were rigorous, and everybody's eyes were on her. She knew that any failure would mean not just that "Patricia Grace Murphy couldn't do it" but that black women couldn't do it.

On one of her flights, she was serving the coach class, when the passenger she was attempting to serve gave her a dirty look and asked, "Don't you know your place?" At first, she didn't even know what to make of the question, but when his expression and his wife's demeanor of embarrassment made his meaning all too clear, Patricia looked at him levelly. "My place is here," she answered, and she stayed firmly in that place for thirty-five years.

Patricia showed everybody that she was in her rightfully-earned place and that African American women could join her there. Delta hired its second black stewardess, Phenola Culbreath-Smith, on October 3, 1966. She, too, had problems finding housing, and because this was in Memphis, segregation kept her even from rooming with a white colleague. The pastor of a local church found a family in his congregation that was willing and able to let her stay with them. There were fifty other flight attendants in Phenola Culbreath-Smith's class; she was the only African American. Like Patricia, she felt the pressure to succeed but the majority of her colleagues welcomed and supported her. For example, she had a layover in Jackson, Mississippi, when there was a great deal of racial tension in the city. The captain of that flight asked the hotel clerk on duty to give her a room on the same floor as his, as close as possible, so that if she experienced any problems, he would be available.

HOWEVER, NOT ALL CREW MEMBERS were as welcoming and some were genuinely hostile. In 1969 Geri Walker, a very pretty, dignified young African American woman, was on a flight from Detroit to Ft. Wayne, working in the first class cabin, which includes serving the captain and copilot in the cockpit. The captain made a very transparent excuse to ensure that Karen, the white flight attendant on the flight, would serve first class. Although Geri agreed, Karen refused point blank, explaining that Geri had seniority, so she should serve first class. He told Karen to do as he said or to get off his plane. She said, "Okay," went to the back cabin, retrieved her suitcase, and got off the plane. At the agent's desk, she explained that the captain had kicked her off the flight for her refusal. The flight had to get special permission to fly with only two flight attendants so that it could leave on time.

Like any other member of the flight crew, the co-pilot was not allowed to disagree openly with the captain, but during the flight, he came out to get the captain's beverages and apologized to Geri for the incident, indicating that he, too, understood why the captain had refused to let Geri serve him.

Once Geri returned to Miami, she was required to report the incident. She described what had happened, adding that everything indicated that the pilot wanted to make sure that a white woman served the cockpit and first class. Karen and Geri saw each other several months later, but they never discussed the unpleasant flight again.

Ann Thomas, another black flight attendant, had a very similar experience with one of her captains later that same year. After takeoff on a flight from Atlanta to Dallas, she knocked at the door of the cockpit and waited to be told to come in, asking what he wanted to drink. His answer came quickly, "I don't allow niggers in my cockpit."

She was too shocked to respond and yet understood that his authority was absolute. Instead of protesting, she simply told the white flight attendants that they would have to tend to the cockpit.

∽o∽

TRAINING HAD ITS INCIDENTS, TOO. Terry Taylor was born in England to a biracial couple; it was much easier for blacks and whites to marry in Europe then. Terry's father fell in love with her mother, an Englishwoman, while serving in the military overseas. During the war, the government didn't make it easy for military men, especially African American soldiers, to bring home war brides. The Virginia vs. Loving case that legalized interracial marriage in all of the United States wasn't settled until 1967. Like me, Terry grew up seeing the world, with a father in the military, and wanted a career that would let her keep traveling.

She started her training on March 2, 1970. When she was settling into her dorm room and hanging up her brand new clothing and shoes from New York, a white stewardess trainee, Jan, walked in and eyed her expensive and stylish clothing. "What's a nigger like you doing with clothes like those?" she asked.

Terry turned around and demanded, "What the hell did you say?" and after not getting a response, ordered, "I think you'd better get the hell out of my room." Terry's roommate, a white former nun, immediately got on her knees and started silently praying, probably for peace.

Her prayers weren't answered immediately. From then on, Jan lost no opportunity to needle her, and, for the most part, Terry chose to ignore them. However, Jan went too far when she decided to take control of the graduation performance. Terry was in charge of a skit in which all of the five black stewardesses had speaking parts, but she wasn't at the rehearsal when Jan, who actually didn't have any authority, took it upon herself to cancel their speaking parts because the skit was "too long."

Vicky Bell, one of the other African American stewardesses, told Terry what had happened and then went to call her mother and confide this insult to her. Jan overheard this and demanded to use the exact phone that Vicky was using, despite the fact that others were available. Vicky closed the telephone booth door (that was when almost all public buildings and major streets had telephone booths with public phones) and thought that the incident was over.

The next day, though, the dorm mother came to Terry's room to tell her she was going to be sent home the next day. That very morning, after one of her classes, Terry received an order to report to Mr. Fontenot's office immediately. He supervised all pilots and stewardesses, not just the trainees. When she came into his office, he told her to sit down. He then shoved a paper in her face, telling her to sign it.

She asked what it was, and he said boldly, "This is your resignation."

"I'm not going to sign anything and I'm not going to resign. I'm graduating in a few days."

He curtly told her that she had been accused of instigating a "race riot." This was about as loaded an accusation as "terrorism" is today. Serious race riots in July and August 1964, the famous Watts riot in 1965, and Martin Luther King's assassination in 1968 had sparked riots in nearly every major city with a large black population.

Terry was flabbergasted but still refused to sign, despite knowing that it was a powerful accusation that would pander to commonly accepted prejudices. She asked to make a call and he let her, even stepping outside the office to let her use the phone in private. Her uncle had told her to call a certain Mr. Clark if she were ever in trouble. She thought that perhaps he was a powerful family friend. Instead, he worked at the Civil Aeronautic Board (CAB) and was in charge of investigating discrimination complaints.

She explained her bewildering situation, saying that she had been told to resign and accused of inciting a race riot. Mr. Clark listened carefully, took notes, and called Delta's CEO, Charles H. Dolson, one of his personal friends. After listening to her side of the story through Mr. Clark, the CEO then called Mr. Fontenot to hear his story.

As it turned out, Jan's father was rumored to be a major shareholder and had called Mr. Fontenot to say, "I don't care what you have to do to take care of this matter, but I don't want my daughter to graduate with that nigger."

Once Mr. Clark knew of this, he called Terry back. "I do not want you to accept the offer to resign."

Terry told him she had no intention of resigning. "I want to graduate with my friends, and I want to fly for Delta. I've earned it." Mr. Clark then called Mr. Fontenot back and told him exactly the kind of trouble that Delta would be in if it persisted in its accusations.

When Mr. Fontenot called her back into his office, she could see from his appeasing expression that things had changed. "Terry, I'm so sorry for all this confusion. What we're going to do is consider you finished with your training. You don't even have to take the final exam. We'll give you a pass to go home and come back in a week so you can march across the stage with the next graduating class."

She knew that this was a compromise, since she had earned the right to march with her own class, but she figured that she had made her point and stood up for herself, so she agreed.

Mr. Fontenot introduced himself, very humbly, at Terry's graduating class and said that she had gotten sick and would have to wait for the next class to march across the stage. All of her friends and those who had heard the story through various channels knew the real reason.

After Terry graduated, she and many other members of her class were assigned to the base in New Orleans. Despite the high population of blacks in the city, landlords who would rent to blacks were hard to find. However, a woman who had recently divorced a pilot and gotten the house (which the pilot was still paying for) in the settlement had a great idea for mingling kindness to the stewardesses and spite toward her ex-husband. She offered to rent rooms in her large and luxurious home to the black stewardesses, knowing exactly how much this would rile him. I'm sure that today she'd have posted a lot of pictures of her revenge on Twitter and Instagram.

NOT ALL BLACK STEWARDESSES WERE SO LUCKY in finding housing or even hotel accommodations. After one flight, the crew all went to the same Mississippi hotel where the airline had made reservations. The senior flight attendant hands in a "sign in" sheet of the attendants' names, in order of seniority, so that the most senior one—in that case, a black woman—gets assigned a room first. The desk clerk looked at the name on her wings and asked, "What do you want?" Despite the protocol of giving the senior flight attendant the first room, he made her wait to be the last.

Sometimes when housing wasn't available, African American stewardesses were made to live with the families of people who worked Cabin Service (cleaning and restocking the planes with beverages, pillows, and ice). They often had to sleep in the children's rooms.

In other cases, there was no housing within the approved distance from the airport. Inez, the base supervisor for New Orleans, had liked Patricia Murphy and helped her leverage her seniority to get an apartment that was actually outside the approved area since that was the only place that would rent to her. Inez had a well-earned reputation for being strict, and many thought she went overboard. She would call stewardesses out in front of everyone if their uniform had the tiniest deviation from the official standards. The rules forbade false eyelashes, and if she noticed a stewardess wearing them, she'd pull them off then and there. (Fortunately or unfortunately, she never made a false identification, pulling some poor woman's real eyelashes off!) But in this case, Inez bent the rules.

Early in Terry's flying career, she and the rest of her stewardess crew were having lunch in the Hilton hotel restaurant in Nashville. A gentleman came to their table, introduced himself as part of the Elvis Presley crew, and asked if they would like to attend the concert in a few hours. Everyone responded with an enthusiastic yes, except Terry and Jackie, the two black stewardesses in the group.

Once he walked away, one of the girls asked Terry why she didn't want to go. Terry said she had heard that Elvis had once said that the only thing that "a Negro can do for me is buy my records and shine my shoes." Terry said she couldn't support anyone that would say anything like that. The girls understood but said they were still going to the concert.

The gentleman came back with the passes and said, "Ladies, the limo is waiting out front for us to leave now for the concert." As Terry and Jackie walked out with them, they could see Elvis Presley standing outside his limo, greeting the girls. He also seemed to notice that Terry and Jackie did not approach the limo and stayed at the hotel.

Upon arriving at the concert, Elvis asked the other stewardesses why they hadn't come. The girls told him the story that Terry had relayed at the table. He became visibly disturbed by this, and once they returned to the hotel, Elvis requested that they go to her room and let her know that he wanted to meet her personally to explain the rumor.

Terry was finally persuaded to get dressed and join them in his suite. When Terry entered his room, Mr. Presley approached her with his hand extended to introduce himself and to apologize for that terrible rumor. He went on to say how he never would have said anything that terrible and did not feel that way. He repeatedly asked her to believe him. She was finally convinced by his sincere and pleasant demeanor and by his apology for the hurt that the rumor caused. She was convinced that he indeed wouldn't say anything of that nature. They remained in the room for about an hour, enjoying the conversation about his life and the drawbacks of being in the limelight. He was casual and entirely at ease, even sitting on the floor next to her.

As far as researchers can tell, the rumor had started way back in 1957, when the magazine *Sepia* had quoted an anonymous source as saying that "Elvis said it once." No other source has ever suggested that this was his attitude and, in fact, people of all races who knew him were willing to go on the record, saying that he never would have said a thing like that. They cited numerous instances in which Elvis went out of his way to spend time with his fans of any color. Certainly, Terry and Jackie were among that number after their encounter with him.

Terry might have been one of the most gentle and ladylike people alive, but she was always ready to stand up for herself. A pilot learned all about her backbone when he looked around as he and the flight crew was standing near the cockpit, and said, not recognizing that Terry is biracial, "Glad there's no niggers on board."

She turned around and demanded, "What the hell did you just say?"

I wasn't there, of course, but I could imagine her voice so hard and uncompromising that it could cut through steel faster than a laser. The pilot gaped for a while, turned red, and then went into the cockpit without another word. But that pilot never said anything about race to her again and didn't come out of the cockpit that entire flight.

⌒o⌒

IN THE EARLY DAYS, FLYING A NORMAL THREE-DAY TRIP, the senior flight attendant got a room to herself, while the other flight attendants shared a double room. We got used to finding some flight attendants uncomfortable with sharing rooms. At times, the senior flight attendant would offer the African American stewardess her single room so that the other white woman wouldn't have to share with the black woman. There was always some excuse, "Oh, we're such good friends; we have a lot to catch up on. We're happy to room together." (Somehow, this never happened when there wasn't a black woman in the mix.)

Other times, even more uncomfortably, we found that the other women were reluctant to use the shower or even the bathroom in general after us. They'd always make an excuse to use the shower and bathroom first, or, if they couldn't be the first, would simply skip it. These were the kinds of things that didn't stand out that much on an individual basis, but when we found that every single one of us had had this happen to us several times, even long after the skies were integrated, it was clear that it was a pattern.

Despite all of this, we kept joining Delta in increasing numbers, and Delta was actively trying to recruit blacks. In the South, for example, Delta paid for advertisements on the backs of fans that black churches distributed to their congregations during the summer, and several of our new colleagues heard about Delta's openings this way. Delta also recruited at historically black colleges and universities.

∽o∾

DURING THE LATE 1960s AND 1970s, many blacks were choosing natural hairstyles or ones that reflected traditional African styles. This was not only a beauty choice but also a cultural statement of black pride and, to some extent, a political statement.

Ann Thomas had worn a stylish and well-maintained Afro to work earlier in 1969, even though Afro hair was not on the approved list of styles. When she arrived to sign in for her scheduled flight, the supervisor told her to report to the stewardess lounge instead of taking the flight that day. The supervisor called a reserve attendant to take that flight and told Ann that she would have to take the day off without pay and not be allowed to fly until she had changed her hairstyle. Ann called the general office and spoke to Mr. Banks, who headed the department that oversaw all the flight attendants. He was very sympathetic and arranged for her at least to get paid for that trip, although she did have to change her hair.

Robin Burns, another of the flight attendants hired later in 1969, had sported a conservative straight hairstyle the day she was interviewed and hired and throughout her training, but when she showed up for her first trip as a fully-fledged stewardess, she was sporting an Afro. She experienced some resistance from her supervisor but remained committed to her choice of hairstyle. Today, it's almost difficult to come up with a shocking hairstyle—dyed Mohawks and words or logos shaved into hair are common sights—so it's hard to describe the impact of her act, foregoing the chemical strengtheners that were practically required for a black woman's hair.

After Robin returned to her home base, she was directed to report to her supervisor, who told her that while passengers and fellow crew members complimented her new hairstyle, it was still not on the approved list. Robin decided to take a stand and defend her hairstyle as perfectly appropriate. She prevailed and now Delta allows a wider variety of hairstyles for all of its flight attendants, allowing any hairstyle that is clean, professional, and well-maintained.

Some might wonder why, of all the possible careers that African American women were bursting into, we wanted to fly so much. The pay certainly wasn't great, but it was excellent pay, especially for new graduates. While we were on call for most of the week, we typically worked only three or four days a week. We were also drawn to the excitement, glamour, and frequent encounters with celebrities. Some of us, too, were attracted by the opportunity to mingle with rich men as potential husbands or boyfriends, and several flight attendants had to leave once they married. As for me, I knew that I just wanted to see the world.

CHAPTER THREE:

Dreams Do Come True

FINALLY, ON JANUARY 17, 1971, my acceptance letter came, saying that Delta Air Lines wanted me as a stewardess. I was to report to their training center in Atlanta, Georgia, on February 1. I must say that I had barely heard of Delta. The only airlines I'd heard of were the bigger ones based in the North, while back then Delta was a regional southern airline.

Delta had actually started as a Louisiana crop-dusting company, flying planes low over farmers' fields to scatter pesticides that would have been too laborious to disperse by hand. C.E. Woolman, then the vice president and general manager, bought it for $40,000 (just over $500,000 in 2014 dollars). He renamed the company Delta Air Services to reflect its Delta Valley origins and began to expand it aggressively, moving to Atlanta, still its headquarters, and taking over another regional airline (Chicago and Southern, aka C&S) in 1953. I did not know then that it would become a major international airline or how much of my life I would spend with it.

I also had no idea of exactly what awaited me as a stewardess. I figured that we'd learn more about the planes, but pretty much all I knew was that stewardesses walked up and down the aisle and served food. I never even thought that it would be my life-long career; like most flight attendants, I saw it as, at most, something I'd do for a few years. Off I dashed to training for four weeks to become that glamorous lady in the sky. Locally, this was big news—I even got my name and picture in the paper.

The first hint I got at how rigorous it would be came with that acceptance letter. It said that we'd be paying for our own uniforms, which would come out of our otherwise generous paychecks, and suggested that we bring approximately $150 in traveler's checks to cover our uniform, laundry, hairstyling, gloves, and miscellaneous expenses during our training process. Gloves were on the way out, but Delta was hanging onto the tradition that respectable women wore gloves. The letter also suggested an alarm clock, which definitely came in handy.

I was mailed a "pass" (form used by airline employees for traveling) and was advised to travel early because flights became heavier later in the day. Some things don't change.

Training would begin at 8:00 p.m. on Sunday evening at the training center, where we'd meet the other thirty-one trainees and Delta representatives as well as Stewardess Trainee Supervisor Mary Lou Rouse, then in her forties. The closing of the letter stated they looked forward to "welcoming you into the Delta Family."

I went out to purchase my very first set of luggage at Woolworth, a national dime store chain, roughly the equivalent of K-Mart. These masterpieces were made of the finest compressed cardboard available, but in a dapper blue. I still have two pieces of that set, and the largest one still holds one of each uniform I wore throughout my Delta career, and the smallest (a 12" x 12" piece that then was called a cosmetics suitcase) holds some of my most precious souvenirs, including the key from a Rosarito, Mexico, getaway that I'll talk about more later.

❧

I WAS ANXIOUS TO SEE AND MEET MY ROOMMATE, a bit apprehensive at the thought that we'd be sharing a room for the next six weeks. She turned out to be a tall, attractive redhead from New Orleans with a very pleasant manner, and so we were both fairly quickly assured that we would get along fine. We briefly shared our stories of how we came to be training as Delta stewardesses.

She was a hippie and her parents thought that was just a bit too free-spirited. Her father exerted some influence to get her hired at Delta, hoping that it would give her more direction and structure in her life. I had encountered several hippies before at the University of Illinois, so her attitudes weren't at all a surprise to me. I did have to adjust to her heavy New Orleans accent, however. I'd never lived in the southern United States, and I was amazed at just how long and drawn out my name was when she said it, or how many extra syllables she managed to insert into Casey.

As it turned out, after she graduated, she was also a bit too much of a free spirit for Delta. Among other transgressions, she created her own uniform by putting together pieces from different uniforms, and so she flew for only about three months. I still have fond memories of her and sometimes wonder what she's doing now.

The next woman I met was Adrian Cooper, another black woman. She was tall, slim, and very, very pretty, walking down the hallway of the training center as though it were a catwalk or as though the paparazzi were going to take photos any moment, in fashionable and expensive-looking gaucho pants and tall boots, trailing four pieces of designer luggage. She stopped and introduced herself and I warmed to her immediately. She told me where her room was and added that her friend and previous classmate at Prairie View A&M University, Davye Mable, would be joining the class. Prairie View is a member of the famous Texas A&M University system and one of the Historically Black Colleges and Universities (HBCUs) in the United States. She had a Texas accent, though not a terribly thick one, and I was starting to feel surrounded by all the different parts of the United States.

Davye showed up about an hour later. She had a short and adorable haircut, huge eyes, and a petite build. Her sense of humor and something a bit impish about her made me think that if Carol Burnett were black, this is what she'd look like.

I met the fourth African American member of our class, Dot Daniels, shortly afterward. She was wearing a short, curly hairstyle and was also extraordinarily pretty. Unlike Adrian and Davye, she looked a bit more quiet and reserved but had one of the most infectious laughs I'd ever had the sheer fun of hearing. She grew up in a small town like me, from a farming family in Shellman, Georgia, and had graduated from another HBCU, Fort Valley State University, also in Georgia.

The four of us bonded immediately, glad to see potential friends. We often met to study for our tests and went out to dinner together. We were all fascinated by one another's different backgrounds and our varied lives before coming together. The idea that all of us came from such different worlds was a taste of the variety and excitement that we knew our careers were going to offer us.

DURING TRAINING ITSELF, WE'D WEAR STREET CLOTHES, including a girdle and hose. Hose were still standard wear for women, but girdles were old-fashioned even then. (Of course, everything comes around, and now women and men wear Spanx, though we call it a "shaper" rather than a girdle.) All of us students found out soon that, yes, they checked, and we got used to the stewardess trainee supervisor coming up behind us every now and again to pinch us to see if our girdles were on. We also had to bring old slacks, socks, and low-heel shoes because we would be performing emergency ditching procedures during our training period.

My hire weight was 120, at 5'4," which was already the maximum allowed. The airlines watched every pound since fuel was so expensive, so the less we weighed, the less we cost. That wasn't as bad as the earliest days, when not only did they weigh the stewardesses and the luggage but the passengers as well.

Some years later, Delta revised the policy and stewardesses were allowed five additional pounds after they turned thirty. Once we were actually flying, we had weight check every month, and if you were one pound over your maximum weight, you were suspended (without pay, of course!) until you brought your weight down. We had our own tricks for this. One person would distract the stewardess supervisor, and a woman whose weight was perfect would go in and sneak a piece of gum in the right place on the scale to make sure that the next woman could get away with a few extra pounds. This sounds like a school prank but it was very serious; if somebody checked in overweight too often, she would be transferred to another department such as Cabin Service (cleaning and restocking the cabin), a humiliating demotion.

The supervisors doing the weigh-ins weren't always pleasant or professional. One of them looked me over after weigh-in and asked where all my weight was, then took another look at my hips and said, "Oh, that's where." We got an extra joy out of tricking those supervisors.

During training, we had classes on makeup and hairstyles, and we emerged from these classes looking rather like clones from a staid fashion magazine. The most acceptable hairstyles were the pageboy or a bun, with pearl stud earrings, even then the most conservative jewelry possible. Technically, we were allowed any other shoulder-length cut as long as it was a "complimentary style." Delta, of course, decided what was complimentary.

These weren't the only rules that flooded into our personal lives, whether we liked it or not (as a pizza and cake lover, I definitely did not). During training, we were not permitted to go to a man's apartment, and curfew was 11:00 on Saturdays nights. Of course, rules were made to be broken, and we did so on several Saturday nights. Dot's boyfriend lived in town, and, so through him, we met lots of locals. I did sometimes go out with young men we met but nothing developed. Adrian also knew some locals, including some handsome young football players, and of course I appreciated meeting them, too.

If we wanted to break curfew, we'd coordinate with one of the other trainees in the dorm who didn't have any Saturday night plans. We would set up the time we expected to return to the dorm, and she would sneak past the dorm mother and down the stairs and unlock the front door after deactivating the alarm. With a whispered "thank you," both the curfew breaker and her accomplice carefully tiptoed back upstairs to our rooms. We knew we were running the risk of being fired, but the lure of the night out on the town (and the thrill of breaking the rules) made the risk seem worthwhile.

⋘∘⋙

TRAINING WAS RIGOROUS, not just because of all of the control over our appearances and personal lives but mentally, physically, and emotionally. None of us had really foreseen that we'd learn the procedures for evacuating an aircraft, how to identify different kinds of fires and know which extinguishers to use and how, or that we'd practice water landings in a pool, which substituted for the lakes or oceans on which we might land in real life. The practice water landings would have been fun as a bonding exercise (hint there to corporate trainers), but our trainers made us recognize that this was a serious matter. We were all sobered when we truly realized that in the case of a water landing or other emergency, we knew where the emergency equipment was and how to use it, and we were responsible for passenger safety and would be called upon to do rescue work.

In rescue situations, we were responsible for identifying passengers who would be able to assist us and for giving them directions. If the situation involved heavy lifting or moving things, we'd be giving orders to men, who would be looking to us to make the decisions and tell them what to do. Today, most people wouldn't think twice about a situation in which a woman has the authority and instructs men on what to do, but then, it was a genuine role reversal.

Our training also included medical needs. We had to learn about what to do for people in diabetic comas, people who had seizures, women going into labor, or passengers who were hyperventilating or having other forms of a panic attack. One of the biggest things that we needed to learn was CPR (cardiopulmonary resuscitation), and we practiced regularly on a life-size dummy.

We had to recognize the signs of a passenger who might be a potential problem, whether it was somebody who was excessively nervous and might have a panic attack, somebody who might become belligerent, or those who appeared to have enough to drink already and shouldn't be served any more alcohol. We also learned how to address even the most basic questions that could come from novice flyers, without changing expression. After her training, Mae Wallace told me of a traveler on one of her flights who assumed that the airplane was like a train and the different sections of the plane would go to different locations. She nervously asked if she was in the right part of the plane to get to her destination.

We polished our skills in the arts of being a sophisticated hostess to our passengers. We had to learn about different wines and which to serve when and how, and the condiments to serve with caviar. (We served black caviar, of course, the most expensive kind.) We learned how to cook beef or prime rib in the galley and carve it in front of the passengers.

We had to maintain a B average in all of these classes, and if we didn't, we'd be dismissed from the training program. The company would give you the farewell present of an airline ticket back to your home town.

We were constantly reminded that we represented Delta and this governed our lives at all times. Above all, we had to be respectable ladies. After training, we weren't allowed to live with a man, unless he was a relation. As long as we were wearing our uniforms, we couldn't even go into an establishment that served liquor, whether or not we actually indulged. Of course, our names could never appear in a newspaper unless the context reflected positively upon us and thus upon Delta.

NOT SURPRISINGLY, OUR CLASS STARTED WITH THIRTY-TWO WOMEN and ended with only twenty-four. Some left because they were unable to maintain a passing average, some left because they were homesick, and others realized they didn't want a career in the aviation field. But the graduating class of February 1971 included me and three other black women.

That was the most exciting month of our lives. We were now hostesses, expected to treat the passengers as though they were guests in our own homes, giving them a pleasant and memorable experience, using all the skills, professionalism, and confidence that we'd acquired.

Our salary was a generous one for the times. During training, we got a meal allowance of $9.10 per day as well as our bimonthly paychecks, and in the 1970s, the starting salary was approximately $11,400 (the equivalent of about $62,000 in today's dollars) during the probationary period, which usually lasted six months. After those six months, we got a raise to $12,840, another raise to $13,680 after a year, and for our second and third years, $14,580 and $15,540 (the equivalent of about $82,000). We had achieved our dream career and had survived the grueling training; we were on our way to becoming stars in the sky.

My first assignment was based in Miami, also my first time living on my own, away from the comfort and security of my parents and siblings. The only reassuring factor was that Dot Daniels and I were based in Miami together; naturally, we decided to become roommates. It was a true comfort for me to know we would be treading unknown waters together.

CHAPTER FOUR:

The Good, the Bad, the Unpleasant

A T THE AGE OF TWENTY-ONE, I was about to have the first experience of my life that I recognized as racism. We moved to Miami, and Delta had arranged for Dot and me to stay at a hotel for seven to ten days, just enough time to secure living accommodations. Each day, we'd eagerly secure a newspaper in search for apartments close to the airport. The first day seemed a little dismal because Dot and I had no luck. We persistently had the misfortune of not showing up early enough to view the apartments. Somehow once we showed up, the landlords told us that the apartment had just been rented. After a while, we started to recognize the pattern and started to suspect what was going on.

We dragged ourselves back to the hotel to exchange stories with the other girls that had also been transferred to Miami. To our chagrin, most of the girls had found vacancies, secured a lease, and were moving into their apartment in the next few days. The ones that hadn't found housing invited us to trek along with them the next day. Once again, when Dot and I appeared at the apartment complexes, there suddenly weren't any vacancies. The white girls would even go before us to start the process. Once Dot and I showed up in person, the landlords said that they couldn't rent the apartment to that many people or they came up with some other ridiculous excuse to refuse us housing. The Fair Housing Act, which prohibits racial discrimination in housing, had passed in 1968, but as far as these landlords were concerned, it didn't even exist.

After a lot of frustrating searching, we finally secured a wonderful apartment in Miami Springs, five minutes from the airport. A lot of other stewardesses from Eastern Airlines and Delta lived in this Stew Zoo. Single men also loved to live in these apartment complexes. Who wouldn't enjoy hanging out at the pool with stewardesses from several airlines while they waited to be assigned their next trips? We loved the single men's presence, too. If we weren't called to the airport by a certain time, we knew that we were free for the rest of the evening, or even for a few days. Having single football players and other athletes, doctors, lawyers, teachers, and pilots, to name just a few of the professions represented there, ensured that there was always something going on, whether it was a party or just a nearly-constant gathering at the pool.

We couldn't drink a certain number of hours before duty, but when we knew that we were free, we often enjoyed cocktails with our neighbors. One of our favorite drinks then was sangria, which we loved not just for the flavor and hint of Spanish exoticism, but because it didn't really matter if we used cheap wine.

Our neighbors included two of the most popular players for the Miami Dolphins. They had some wild and crazy parties in their two-bedroom apartment, with any number of groupies hanging around these young, handsome, single athletes. At some of the parties, the groupies all but took numbers and stood in line just to have some personal time with them. One of these players used to joke with me all the time about whether I was ready to enjoy some private time with him, too. Neither one of us took it seriously, however.

WE WEREN'T SAFE FROM RACISM, though, even in this Stew Zoo community. Geri Walker had once called a cab the night before for one of those "O (oh) dark hundred" pickups. Since it was coming from Stew Zoo and at that hour, the cab driver was expecting a stewardess. However, when he saw Geri, he took off, leaving her standing on the sidewalk with her bags and with no way to get to the airport, even though she was waving frantically, hoping against hope that somehow he just hadn't seen her. She could only go back inside, call another cab from another company, and hope that this driver one would do his job.

We got used to that and always allowed extra time for the driver to notice our race and, if he drove on without picking us up, to call another cab and not be late for work. This was not only inconvenient but also infuriating, that we had to manage our lives and establish our daily routines around their prejudices.

We also had the unnerving experience of turning on the local news station and seeing a report of a burning cross being thrown on Palmetto Expressway, behind our apartment complex. We knew that Miami is part of the South and that this kind of thing was far from rare, but somehow knowing that it happened so near our home made the reality too close for comfort. But for the most part, we loved our Stew Zoo and our exciting new lives.

MY OWN FIRST FLIGHT, IN FEBRUARY 1971, though, can be described only as a horrible flying disaster. It was a full flight from Miami to New York, and there were two other attendants who clearly were close friends. They stuck together and left me to work the tourist cabin alone. Something in their demeanor made me suspect that this was because of my race rather than because I was the new kid on the block.

I was already nervous on my first flight, alone in the tourist cabin, with every single person expecting to be the first one to be served and more than ready to have a tantrum when they weren't. If you have a choice between a) dealing alone with a cabin full of call bells and demanding passengers and b) having a tooth extracted, I'm telling you, call your dentist and say goodbye to that tooth. The pain won't last as long, and the dentist will at least leave enough blood in your body for you to survive.

Those passengers wanted every drop of blood in my body, but, at least at the dentist, you don't have to smile ear to ear and ask the equipment how you can help it. I managed to keep my smile on, my hair neat, and my makeup on my face until we hit clear air turbulence—that is, turbulence with no warning. As I was passing a meal tray to the person sitting at a window seat, I lost my balance and grip on the tray and dropped it right onto the woman who was sitting in the center seat. She was wearing a beautiful white silk suit, which she certainly hadn't wanted to have updated with a brand new coffee stain. She didn't scream at me or make a scene, but she was clearly very angry. I wanted to crawl under one of the seats and hide.

I was almost ready to break down after this embarrassing accident. However, I learned that sometimes angels take the plane. Some pilots from a small private company who happened to be passengers on that flight saw just how close I was to losing it entirely and decided to take pity on me. They both got out of their seats, and one of them positioned himself in the galley while the other one helped me bring the trays in the back galley to be placed in the tray carriers for storage.

Even with their help, I wasn't quite sure that the flight ever would end or that I'd ever get away from the woman with the "new" brown and white silk suit. The flight finally did land, and the woman left the aircraft. I had time to redo my makeup and to consider, gloomily, whether or not this was really the right life for me. I decided that I'd come this far and that it was far too early to give up.

On my next flights, fortunately, I learned that my first experience wasn't typical and that most crews were more like those two angels who came to help. I learned that I could expect help and support and that it was easy to become friends with other crew members.

That isn't to say that there weren't the occasional tensions. We all had to adjust to constantly meeting new co-workers and being on different teams all the time. Everybody had their own way of doing things, even something as simple as setting up the beverage cart. But in an atmosphere where we were expected to get everything perfect, especially in first class, and where colleagues each had a different notion of the best way it should be done, we sometimes got into conflicts like where the orange juice should go, on the right or left side of the soda.

The thing about working on an airplane was that we couldn't just ignore one another or agree to disagree. There's only one beverage cart and only one galley, and we had to work physically close together. Even more than that, collectively we were responsible for the well-being of the passengers and for giving them a pleasant experience. If we had personality conflicts, we couldn't afford to let the passengers, or even the pilot, get a hint of it, so we learned to get along.

CHAPTER FIVE:

May I Have Your Attention – The First Star Has Boarded

T HERE WERE SO FEW BLACK STEWARDESSES that it made for an almost immediate bond when we met one another. While walking down the rotunda in the Hartsfield Airport, now known as the Hartsfield–Jackson Atlanta International Airport, in 1971, I spotted a tall African American stewardess sporting a well-maintained short haircut and pretty enough to need just a touch of makeup to enhance her beauty. As we got closer, she smiled and said, "Hi, I'm Patricia, how are you doing?" It turned out that this was Patricia Grace Murphy, the first black stewardess Delta hired on June 27, 1966. That first exchange of pleasantries and smiles created a bond of unspoken approval and pride for each other at being pioneers.

Most stewardesses bonded easily, especially black stewardesses, because there were so few of us and our race gave us so many common experiences. In strange cities, stewardesses found a lot of comfort in familiar faces and tended to live in the same parts of town, close to the airport. Many of us had gone to the same schools or recognized others as friends of friends. We also bonded over our shared responsibilities, exchanged secrets for surviving some new challenges, and swapped stories about some delightful experiences or horror stories. That established a quick camaraderie, but these bonds often developed into deeper friendships, especially because we faced unique burdens.

Those of us who started integrating the skies always wanted to know how many other blacks were in our training classes or, in later years, how many were on a flight together. We were all proud of the running tally of other women like us who were being hired and joining us. Sure enough, that was Patricia's next question. I proudly answered "three others." Patricia and I made mental notes of the growth in the numbers, wished each other a safe and pleasant trip, and said that we hoped to see one another again soon.

∽o∾

IN LATE 1971, WHEN I WAS THE ONLY BLACK PERSON ON THE CREW, I had my own very unpleasant experience, waiting for my room assignment at a hotel in North Carolina. I watched other crew members (captain and other pilots always get their rooms first) get their keys and go to their assigned rooms, heading to the elevator. When I got my key, though, the desk attendant said, "We don't have any more rooms left in this part of the hotel. Your room is in the back and an outside room."

Delta's policy, though, was to book everybody on the same floor, if possible keeping all the women close together. So there I was in a strange town, strange location, and walking in the dark to my room alone. It made me feel unsafe, even in my room, and that was when I started being extra cautious about my personal safety in hotels where I thought I might encounter hostility. I'd check the closets and behind the shower curtain and put my own portable lock or a door wedge, which I always carried in my suitcase, on the door before I'd unpack or relax.

Before you think that I was being paranoid, this was a time when hotel locks weren't especially secure. There were almost never deadbolts; in fact, most doors were fairly easy to open with a credit card (which travelers who were in the habit of losing keys took advantage of). There was also no such thing as a key card and often travelers left with the physical keys to their rooms, either by accident, as a souvenir, or, sometimes, to come back and look for valuables while the next guest was out. In those days, there were no video cameras or cell phones that we could use if the room phone wasn't working. Today's hotel rooms are much more secure, and now when I check the closets and the bathroom and put my suitcase in front of the door, it's mostly just an old habit that I never broke.

Airline crews also have their own full supply of urban legends, and a lot of these are about flight attendants found murdered in their rooms, being attacked by somebody who jumped out from behind the shower curtain, or, of course, the famous story about a flight attendant being found under the bed many days (or weeks) after being murdered in the room. In most cases, these were just urban legends, but there were real stories about flight attendants being kidnapped or murdered, and there are stories about them later in this book.

$$\infty 0 \infty$$

BUT WHILE WE HAD THESE WORRIES, we also enjoyed the excitement of our lives and of course we met many single men. My roommate Dot and I had been invited to Los Angles for a weekend by our neighbor who played for the Dolphins. While we were out at a club, one of his friends came over to greet him. He introduced us to this tall handsome man wearing jeans, a tailored shirt, and a great smile. "Casey, Dot, this is Fred Williamson."

"Hi, ladies," he said and then continued a brief conversation with Dick, leaving a few minutes later. Fred Williamson, a former professional American football defensive back, was one of the first African American male action actors, specializing in the blaxploitation or blacksploitation genre that was just getting started in the United States.

It wasn't long before another tall, handsome, and boyish-looking man, another friend of Dick's, came by our table. After the introduction, he asked if we would mind if he joined us. He and I ended up talking for quite some time and before the night ended, we had exchanged phone numbers. He called me later that week in Miami, and we made plans to get together in a few weeks back in Los Angeles. The relationship lasted about two years, and I'm sorry to say that it didn't end as romantically as it began. In fact, I'm going to call him James to protect his identity.

He was one of the most charming men I had ever met, and by then, I had met several. We dined at some of the most expensive restaurants in Los Angeles, took trips to Rosarito, Mexico, (which then was a very fashionable getaway) for romantic beachfront hotel rooms and shopping, and did all the other kinds of things that would make a wonderful montage in a romantic comedy. Even his career as a movie and television producer was glamorous. Things were going well, and I must say I had grown comfortable in this blissful relationship, which is why I certainly wasn't expecting this kind of ending.

I was packing my bags after one of my trips to his home in LA and found a bottle of fingernail polish that I hadn't remembered leaving. I figured, though, that since it was one of my favorite colors, I must have left it. In hindsight, I should have seen more in that.

On another trip, I was watching his two little girls (six and eight) so he could get some rest before going out to dinner that evening. One of his girls asked me if I knew her daddy's girlfriend, which of course confused me since I thought I had sole ownership of that position. I asked a few questions, pretending not to be concerned. "No, I don't know her. What's her name?"

"Judy," she said as she drew a heart in his shag carpet. I was starting to see the irony in that.

"Oh, is she nice?" I asked and got an immediate, "Yes, she took us to a football game and bought us candy."

After that, she realized that maybe this was information I wasn't supposed to know. To help ease us out this awkward situation, I asked them if they wanted something to eat and made them sandwiches. After getting them settled at the table with their snack, I excused myself and stormed into the bedroom where Prince Charming was resting, looking all dazed with sleep.

I said it was time to get up, and, in the softest tone I could muster, trying to conceal my anger, I asked," So, James, who is Judy?"

"Uh, uh, what did you say, Casey?"

"Who is Judy?" As he stuttered and tried to come up with a good lie, I said, "Get your ass up and take care of your own kids. I'm leaving."

It was a great exit line, but now how do you really leave someone who lives in North Hollywood Hills, when you don't have a car or even a bike, can't call a cab, and your closest friend lives near the LAX airport? So, I did the next best thing: I walked down the hill, went to the nearest grocery store, and called my big sister in Chicago to inform her about this disturbing situation.

When she answered, I blurted out, "James's daughter just got his ass busted." We talked for awhile because I wanted to stay long enough for James to worry whether or not I had really found a way to leave him. As I started to venture back up the hill, I realized that locating his house was an adventure: too many curves, left turns, right turns, and dead-end streets.

By the time I was hopelessly lost, a familiar red Corvette pulled up. Now from the concerned look on his face, I felt I had made him suffer enough. Deep down I was thinking, "Thank you, Jesus, he found me." I was certainly relieved to have been rescued. On the way back to his place, he did try to say that I hadn't understood the situation. I didn't quite believe him, but at the time I wasn't quite ready to end the relationship, especially because on the ride back to his place, he apologized repeatedly and said how worried he was when I left and he couldn't find me anywhere nearby. We hadn't talked about a future together or about marriage, so while I definitely felt betrayed, it didn't feel like the relationship was broken beyond repair.

However, I was much more alert to possible signals than before. On another time he was flying to Atlanta for a business trip. I knew which hotel he'd be staying in, so I called him. I was surprised when a woman answered the phone, "Hi, this is Judy."

I asked who she was and she answered, "I'm James's girlfriend."

"Oh, so am I." I took a cab to the hotel and the two of us were waiting for him when he came to take Judy to dinner. While he started the evening with (at least) two girlfriends, when the evening was over, he had two fewer.

❦

MONTHS LATER AS I WAS BOARDING MY FLIGHT, walking toward me was this gorgeous 6'4" man. He had striking light hazel eyes and wore a full Afro. We made eye contact, and he flashed the most perfect smile I had ever seen. Then and there, I knew I was to move on to a new adventure, my broken heart completely healed from my experience with James.

He was the first to speak—I was still too busy looking at him. "Hi, my name is Greg. How are you?"

I managed to get through introducing myself and the usual pleasantries. We smiled at each other even more, he went to his seat, and we took off for Detroit.

After the beverage service, Greg asked me where I was based and if I was laying over in Detroit. I said yes, and he offered his phone number and asked to take me to dinner that night. Unfortunately, my layover was too short, but I gave him my number and promised that next week I would be back on a longer layover and would love to go to dinner then.

He called me later that week when I was staying at my apartment in the Miami Stew Zoo, and we chatted for awhile, getting to know one another, and made plans for my next trip to Detroit. As we chatted, we realized we had a number of things in common and enjoyed talking.

The two weeks until I'd next be in Detroit seemed to take much longer than that, but finally I was there. Greg picked me up from the hotel, and we had a wonderful dinner and free-flowing conversation the whole evening. The romantic spark wasn't there after awhile, but we very much enjoyed one another's company and became good friends. I always looked forward to Detroit layovers when we could spend some time together.

One night, back home in Miami, as I was putting groceries away, I got a phone call. A very pleasant voice asked, "May I speak to Casey?"

"This is Casey speaking."

"Hello, Casey, you don't know me. My name is Rudy. I'm one of Greg's fraternity brothers. He gave me your phone number since I just moved to Miami, and he said I should give you a call as another newcomer here."

We talked about everything for almost three hours, and he finally asked when we could meet face to face. I gave him my schedule for the next two weeks, which happened to be very full. Apparently, that was too long, so he asked if he could come over in the next hour.

I'd enjoyed every minute of the conversation. He was interesting, a great conversationalist, intelligent and funny, and the three hours flew by. I was intrigued and invited him to come by, but explained that it could be for only a few minutes because I had an early check-in. Claiming an early check-in is a flight attendant's "drop and roll" escape mechanism to get out of a bad date, since that was before we had cell phones and could text a friend to call us with a fake emergency.

An hour later, there was a knock on the door. I peeked through the peephole and saw not one but two young men standing in the hall. Before opening the door, I whispered to Dot, my roommate, "I hope he's the one on the right. He is really nice looking."

I opened the door but as usual with unknown visitors, we didn't let them into our apartment, and instead came out to meet them in the hall. It wasn't exactly typical Southern hospitality but we decided better to be safe than sorry.

The visit lasted only about thirty minutes, as both he and I were mostly just interested in seeing one another face to face, and I actually did have an early trip. He had brought his roommate along as a quick escape excuse in case there was no chemistry in person, but we were both definitely interested in one another even more after meeting in person.

When I was next in Miami, about a week later, we had our first official date, and after that, we were together every day that I was in town. It was only two more weeks before he proposed, and we got married exactly a year after the day we met, in 1973. I put in for a base transfer from Miami to Chicago, where he worked as a buyer for Sears, and we bought a house in the suburbs.

We were both twenty-four years old, and, in hindsight, we weren't ready for marriage and for all of the adjustments and changes that marriage brings. My career was a major part of this, as I found it difficult to adjust to needing to coordinate my schedule with anybody else's. My schedule was impossible to plan far in advance, so we could never make definite plans for spending time together, and some weeks it seemed as though I was gone more often than I was home. Other times when I was on reserve, I'd be called in the middle of the night and out of the house in an hour to be gone for three days.

For flight crews, these absences are a fact of life. It takes a certain kind of person to be able to live with a partner with this kind of schedule. We both worked at it, but we divorced four years later, amicably. To this day, I still remember him with affection and deep respect.

∾o∾

ASIDE FROM MY REGULAR FLIGHTS, I was also attending more trainings, as many as I could. While most promotions were based on seniority, some required successful completion of supervisory training. In addition, this was a very innovative time in aviation and so new models of planes were coming out in response to demand. Each time Delta bought a new model of plane, they offered training in its new safety features and in how to best arrange service. These trainings were all voluntary, but if you wanted to be able to fly certain routes, you had to be trained on that particular model of plane.

The first planes I flew were mostly the McDonnell Douglas DC-8-51s, which could seat one hundred and seventy-nine passengers; the Convair CV-880, which had a capacity of one hundred and ten passengers; and the DC-8-61, which could seat two hundred and twelve. But in the early and mid-1970s, thanks to new developments in aviation and to increased demand, there were new wide-body planes coming out, and so I was soon attending training on models like the 747 and DC-10.

While Delta was based in Atlanta, I heard that Chicago was its test kitchen. If Delta wanted to implement a new service and wasn't sure if it was actually possible, they'd assign it to the Chicago base to get it done. If there was a way to do it, the Chicago team would find that way.

The first secret to our success was that we all made a point of knowing the planes inside and out, so everybody was able to envision how something might work out. The second part was that, while we considered the guidelines that came from Atlanta to be perhaps more flexible than Atlanta really had in mind, we were comfortable enough with our expertise, one another, and our shared skills to improvise and to come up with new ways of doing things. By now, our diversity was strength as well. While that was before "innovation" was the big buzzword that it is now, we had the key ingredients in place and were doing it all the time.

Chicago would develop and fine-tune the services, and other in-flight leaders (the team supervisors on the plane) would add their input.

In one example, they wanted us to find a way to change the service flow so that we never blocked both aisles at once by the service carts. This might sound trivial, but when you're trying to complete a full beverage and meal service in a little over an hour to over two hundred and fifty hungry and thirsty people, it's important to be on the same page to complete the seemingly impossible mission. Depending on the plane configuration and the number of passengers, sometimes we weren't able to perform a service without blocking both aisles, but we were able to come up with ways to avoid it under most circumstances and mitigate the inconvenience those times we had to have both aisles blocked.

On the other hand, sometimes we couldn't do things. Delta wanted us to serve a particular full-course meal on a specific flight. We tried every variation we could, from beverage-first to meal-first to simultaneous, but no matter what we tried, we had to tell passengers to stop eating and put their meal trays under their seats to prepare for landing. Not the ending for the elegant meal that Delta wanted to serve! By that time, they respected our abilities enough to know that if we said it couldn't be done, it couldn't be done, unless we got a time machine.

Thanks to this training and to my increasing seniority, I was frequently the flight leader for my trips. In 1975, I also was offered a promotion to become a supervisor on the ground in Chicago. I had mixed feelings about this. On the one hand, it was an honor, and I appreciated the fact that they thought so highly of me that they asked me to do it. On the other hand, this was more like a nine to five job, and I wouldn't fly and see the world in the same way that I had done before. I went through the interviews, pondered the pros and cons for quite some time, talked about it with others, and decided to decline. I had to refuse delicately, so as not to offend anybody or seem ungrateful, but they understood that for me, flying and interacting with the passengers was the heart of my career.

WE MET ALL KINDS OF FAMOUS PEOPLE then because those were the days when private jets were only for the very, very richest or for high level government officials. Some of these encounters were amusing—for example, when Ron Ely, famous for playing Tarzan, was on one of my flights, we started to talk cooking and recipes, and he demanded my beer-marinated fried chicken recipe. Others were more serious.

We met Dr. Martin Luther King Sr. on a flight in the mid-1970s. He came into the galley and struck up a conversation with us that mixed gentle flirtation and more serious discussion of the troubles the country was still experiencing, along with stories about his son and about his own life.

We also met people in the airport, including Muhammad Ali, who joked with me and my roommate Dot, telling her, "Dot, Dot, like the farmer said to the potato, 'Plant you now, dig you later.'" (I heard later that on another flight, he didn't want to put on his seatbelt and told the stewardess, "Superman don't need no seatbelt." Without missing a beat, she told him, "Superman don't need no airplane." Admitting that he was trying to punch above his weight, Ali meekly buckled his seatbelt.

We recognized most celebrities fairly easily, but some we nearly missed. Once one of the other flight attendants came up to me and said quietly, "That's Jimmy Carter, sitting in 11A." That was when Carter was running for president, and, especially because he was sitting in coach class and didn't draw any attention to himself, it took us a long time to recognize him. I got to meet him more formally decades later. In the early 1990s, Delta was a sponsor for President Jimmy Carter's annual fundraiser through the Carter Center for scholarships for low-income children in the Atlanta area. A supervisor invited me to help host the event. It was a pleasure to meet Jimmy and Rosalyn Carter.

I also almost entirely missed another celebrity. There was a very quiet older gentleman sitting in first class, and I was rather indignant that his family would let such a quiet and possibly fragile older man travel alone. I asked him several times if he wanted something to drink or some peanuts. He always smiled warmly and answered with a quiet, "No, thank you. I'm fine." Then, at the end of the flight, he got up, and his entire persona changed. He had seemed rather bent and even frail while he was sitting, but once he was on his feet, he was clearly full of vigor, and that was when we realized that this man was the Duke. To be specific, Duke Ellington, the foremost figure in big-band jazz, one of the most important musical figures of the twentieth century, equally talented at composing, conducting, and playing jazz piano. Usually, we recognized (or somebody among the flight attendants recognized and spread the word) our famous guests, but in this case, his quiet demeanor kept us all in the dark. In any case, we could absolutely believe the story that he acquired the nickname "Duke" for his gentlemanly ways and distinguished demeanor.

As private planes became more common and the respective salaries of sports and entertainment figures increased, these encounters decreased in number over the years. Planes also became less spacious, except in first and business classes, making flying commercial less tempting for celebrities.

CHAPTER SIX:

Coffee, Tea or –

W HILE THE PLANES WERE CHANGING, so were the flight crews. By then, there were more blacks on the flight crews, including in the cockpit, and there were also some Hispanic and Asian crew members. In the 1970s, more and more women were entering careers that previously had been considered mostly men's domains. Women were becoming engineers, architects, and doctors.

In the air, we were expected to be pleasant and professional, but a lot of passengers clung to the image of the stewardess offering, "Coffee, tea, or me?" That was back in the days when "sexual harassment" didn't even exist as a term and when women were expected to shrug off sexism or to take unwanted sexual attention as compliments.

On the one hand, we were chosen to be stewardesses based on our looks and ability to be charming. Many of us were single and interested in meeting the many eligible young men among our passengers. Many of them were interested in meeting us, too.

Today, professionals go to networking events and are delighted to come home with a handful of business cards. As often as not, flight attendants disembarked from flights with more than a couple of business cards, too, but from potential dates rather than potential employers. To be polite, we accepted them all, but most of us had our own system of filing them. If anybody who discreetly slipped me a card had a suspicious band of pale skin on his ring finger, the card went into my left-hand pocket as a short-term stop on its way to the trash. If I was interested, I'd discreetly pencil a note or two of my own to remind me of exactly who the guy was and file it in my right-hand pocket.

We also experienced quite a bit of harmless courtly flirting, meant as a compliment, usually from men who were simply enjoying it as a game. We played along in good spirits, all the while maintaining our "you can dream but you can't touch" demeanor.

On the other hand, virtually every flight attendant experienced ogling or unwanted touching. This was especially common with passengers who had had a few drinks. Usually the passengers stopped after being told to, but sometimes they didn't, and this was always unpleasant.

The good thing is that because we were charged with passenger safety, this gave us the authority to tell them that they were committing a federal offense by interfering with the execution of our duties. We always had the rest of the crew and Delta backing us in case an offender persisted.

We were at some risk just by the nature of our jobs. Before the days of online dating, people mostly met their future dates and partners at school, at work, through friends, or in organizations such as churches. This meant that people got a chance to know one another with some context; you knew exactly who you were meeting. On a flight, you had only a very little time with an attractive stranger and had no idea if he was who he said he was, or if his pleasant demeanor was an act.

While there was a good deal of harmless flirtations, there was also a darker side. In more than a few cases, men got away with lying about their marital status. Flight attendants were virtual strangers, so it was easy to get away with lies. If we lived in the same community, we'd have a lot more clues, know more about the person's background, maybe have friends in common, or probably meet through mutual friends. We met people outside that context, which made things seem very glamorous and exciting but also had a potential for darker things happening.

"Joe," a famous R&B singer, now deceased, was one of many known for throwing his shirt into the audience during his performance and for women throwing their underwear on stage.

When he was on one of my flights, we struck up a conversation. I said that I had no idea why anyone would want to have his smelly sweaty t-shirt. He laughed and said he had to give his audience what they wanted. He also said that he would be in Chicago along with his girlfriend. By chance, his girlfriend knew a close friend of mine. The week came for his show, and I received a phone call from his girlfriend about where they would be staying and setting a lunch date for us to meet.

When I first entered the hotel room, he seemed very pleasant, though still exhausted from the previous night's performance. When I suggested that we pick a place for lunch, his personality seemed to change. He stopped smiling and became very serious. In a matter-of-fact tone, he said that we actually would order from any place in the city rather than go out. After we agreed, even though I said I couldn't stay long, he said that he just wanted to talk some more, and then he resumed his pleasant demeanor.

That was when I noticed some white powder on the dresser next to a pack of cigarettes. He saw me noticing and offered me some, but I turned him down, said that I'd use the restroom and leave, because it was getting late.

When I returned, things had moved quickly, and his girlfriend was already in bed with him. The other thing that had moved was my purse, which was missing. Joe lifted up the covers, exposing their naked bodies and my purse. I asked for the purse, he said, teasingly, "Come get it." Joe pulled me down and tried to make me put my hand under the covers. I was finally able to retrieve my purse without touching anything else and made a very hasty retreat to the exit. I just got my hand on the door knob, and he grabbed me and tried to force me back into the room. What had seemed like a friendly lunch invitation had turned into a cat and mouse game, and he was definitely amused by my attempts to escape. Finally, I got him to rest a minute, dashed to the door, and got out once he was off guard.

OF COURSE, THERE WERE ANY NUMBER OF MEETINGS that all parties thoroughly enjoyed and virtually every single flight attendant met very pleasant dates, some of which flourished into relationships. Sometimes it even led to marriages. Isaiah Thomas (the one who played for the Detroit Pistons in the 1980s, not the one who plays for the Sacramento Kings) met his wife Lynn Kendall on Delta, and Bryant Gumbel (the television journalist and sportscaster) met his first wife June Baranco the same way. Terry Taylor married Bruce Taylor, the defensive back for the San Francisco 49ers, the 1970 Rookie of the Year. Terry and Bruce invested wisely and became the owners of eighteen Burger Kings in Chicago and Seattle, and now they enjoy retired life in Florida.

Pilots and flight attendants often dated and sometimes the passion got overwhelming. A retired pilot friend of mine mentioned that there were more than a few times on those long coast-to-coast flights when the flight attendant would let herself into the cockpit and put a blanket on the floor, where she and the pilot would put a whole new world of meaning into the term "cockpit." (If you ever wanted to know the real origin of the term "cockpit," it actually comes from the disgusting old "sport" of cockfighting. The cockpit was where the birds were forced to fight. The British Navy adopted the term to reference any kind of control area for a vessel. Eventually, the term spread to aviation.) I asked him what on Earth he did during those occasions. "Just kept looking straight ahead," he answered. The autopilot was engaged, and there was no danger but plenty of knowing snickers when the flight attendant emerged later, smoothing her clothing and hair back into place.

There were also plenty of incidents with passengers joining the Mile High Club. Sometimes there was a lot of banging and bumping coming from one of the bathrooms. We always figured people had to be pretty desperate to get it on in there, but some people just want membership to those exclusive clubs, even if they might need a chiropractor to get out. The cabin wasn't immune, either. I was walking through the cabin to do a routine check and found that somebody else was already offering service, at least to her husband. They were so involved that neither of them noticed me standing there. After a moment's consideration, I reached up, opened the overhead bin, grabbed a blanket, threw it over the lady's head, and continued on my way. By my next walkthrough, she was sitting up with her head on his shoulder, and both of them were deeply asleep. Mission accomplished!

Sometimes flight attendants inducted passengers into the club. During a layover, some flight attendants were sharing their most adventurous stories over dinner in a wonderful little Frankfurt restaurant. One told a story of how, during a flight, she and one passenger, the lead singer of a reggae band, caught each others eyes. After takeoff, he asked (as if he didn't know!) how one joined the Mile High Club. She pointed him to the bathroom and told him that if he waited there, she'd join him and show him the requirements.

Delta's repeated mantra was that we should always treat passengers as though they were guests in our own home. However, this kind of special friendliness was against regulations and would have led to strict disciplinary action if anybody reported it. To the best of my knowledge, nobody ever reported anybody else, and as long as the participants were discreet and never did anything that could affect passenger safety or comfort, nothing happened.

Janet Harmon Waterford Bragg
1907-1993
(Pioneer African-American Female Pilot—Chicago, IL)

Bessie Coleman
1892-1926
(The First Black International Pilot in the World)

ROBBINS HISTORIC 1931 AIRPORT

The first airport in the USA built, owned & operated by two African-Americans
Cornelius R. Coffey and John C. Robinson in Robbins, Illinois, County of Cook

This picture of Robbins historic Airport Hangar & Challenger Aero Club pilots was taken in 1933. This Airplane Hangar was large enough to house three airplanes. It was located at 140th PL. and Lawndale Av. in Robbins. The Airport opened in 1931 (Depression years), but in May of 1933 a violent windstorm roared through Robbins completely destroying the hangar and the three airplanes housed inside. For lack of funds the hangar was not rebuilt. Coffey and Robinson excepted an offer to relocate the Aero training school to the 87th & Harlem Airport in Chicago, IL where it remain until the early 50's..

Courtesy of Harold Hurd and Robbins Historical Society & Museum -rev.Jan, 2000

Patricia Banks Edmiston

Patricia Grace Murphy

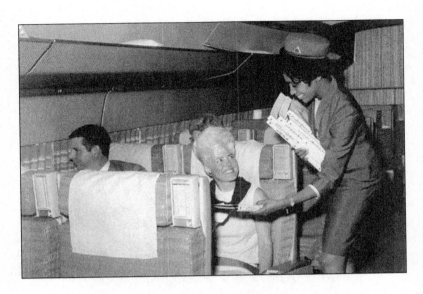

Phenola Culbreath-Smith

Eugene Harmond

Dot Daniels and Casey Grant

Casey Grant's stewardess graduation class

Eric and Rubye Grant (Casey's parents) on their wedding day

The four Grant siblings: Jackie Hardmon, Eric Grant, Casey, Debbie Sanchez

Casey and Eric with Alice Coachman, displaying her 1948 Olympic gold medals

Sharon Hirtzer, Debbie Phillips, Casey Grant, and Ellen Lucas with Smokey Robinson

Rosalynn and Jimmy Carter

Casey, Martin Luther King, Sr., and JoAnn Horne

CHAPTER SEVEN:

A New Development

WHILE IT GOT FAR LESS PUBLICITY THAN THE WOMEN'S MOVEMENT, men were also entering new careers, and in 1973, Delta hired its first male stewards.

Just like Delta hired the most physically attractive and personable female attendants it could, it hired men who looked like models and were intelligent and capable of charming a brick. The job was appealing to men for the same reasons as it was for women—good pay, the opportunity to travel and see the world, and a flexible, if unpredictable work schedule that allowed for stretches of off time that could last for four or six days, which more than compensated for those "O dark hundred" calls.

The first flight attendant was a male, Heinrich Kubis, and his first flight was in 1912, for the German firm Delag, on a Zeppelin flight. He was actually on the Hindenburg during that great aviation disaster and helped several passengers and members of the crew escape. However, the first commercial airplanes were much smaller than Zeppelins—they could hold only about fifteen people, including the pilot and copilot—so the copilot would serve lunch and help airsick passengers.

Those flights were very bumpy, especially because planes couldn't then go above the clouds to escape turbulence, and passengers got sick regularly, especially because flying was so new. The flights were long, too, with the Chicago to San Francisco route, for example, taking about twenty hours. The copilots doubtlessly thought it was a wonderful idea to hire stewards who would have sole responsibility for the passengers and whatever sicknesses they might experience.

The first female flight attendant, Ellen Church, was a pilot and a registered nurse. She wanted to fly professionally but Boeing Air Transport, though it refused to hire her because of her sex, did consider her idea that passengers would feel safer with a registered nurse on board. In 1930 they hired her as head stewardess, and she hired seven other nurses. They all had to be single, under the age of twenty-five, weigh less than one hundred and fifteen pounds, and be 5'4" or shorter. (Planes were smaller then and every pound counted in getting a plane airborne.)

Their responsibilities also included technical ones like helping to refuel the aircraft, adjusting the altimeters, and even helping the pilots to push the aircraft into the hangars. They also had to make sure that passengers didn't stick their arms or heads out the windows, or even throw things. Stewardesses also had to personally guide each passenger who needed a lavatory break, as the emergency exit and the lavatory were right next to one another, and the lighting was not good.

While an automobile accident ended Ellen Church's career as a flight attendant after only eighteen months, she and her colleagues demonstrated the value of the role. Her hometown of Cresco, Iowa, named its municipal airport in her honor.

ᥫᩚ๐ᥫᩚ

NOT ALL AIRLINES FOLLOWED BOEING'S LEAD. Eastern and Pan Am hired men only until WWII, when almost all able-bodied men were either in the military or in vital jobs supporting the war effort, so they had to hire women. (It's a shame that this didn't get as much publicity as Rosie the Riveter, or we could have had Sharon the Stewardess.)

Delta hired its first male flight attendants, Ted Lemon and Richard Black, in 1972, and they started work on January 2, 1973. For us, this meant a great new year. Aside from the pleasure of working alongside these wonderful men, we could also get their help with the heavy lifting, dealing with irate passengers who often treated men more respectfully than women, and reaching things that were stored high. We weren't shy about asking men for help or in expressing our appreciation for them, nor did we mind having them as neighbors in our Stew Zoos.

Many of these men were homosexual, though none of them was entirely out. Of course, the stereotype of gay flight attendants existed then, and some of them, while not out, did very little to conceal their orientation. This disturbed some of the pilots. One used to grumble that he didn't want "queers or night riders [blacks]" in his cockpit. He retired early, and, while of course Delta didn't announce why he left, rumor had it that it was because his colleagues reported his behavior.

Most, however, didn't open up until we had developed a real friendship. This was fairly typical of the times. Most gay men, regardless of race, kept their orientation entirely hidden from the public. Some homosexual men, including black men like Langston Hughes or Bayard Rustin, had small social enclaves or

86

worked in organizations where their orientation could be an open secret, but they could still go to jail for homosexuality and several did.

We tended to become very protective of one another, not just because of the friendships that we developed, but also because we recognized that as minorities, we had a good deal in common. One of these gay men, Fred, became a hero to us and to Delta in general because of his clever thinking and bravery during a potential life or death hijacking situation that I'll go into more detail about later.

LATER IN 1973, THE FIRST AFRICAN AMERICAN MALE FLIGHT ATTENDANT JOINED US. Eugene Harmond was a tall and handsome Smokey Robinson look-alike. He was single and very much enjoyed the opportunities that working around so many eligible young women provided. Eugene had actually gone to Eastern Airlines employment office to apply for a job as a "stewardess" (as they were still called), and he figured that as long as Delta's office was right next to Eastern's, he might as well submit an application there, too. He never heard from Eastern, but a few weeks later, he got his acceptance letter from Delta.

The letter told him to report to the training center and to bring a dark blazer and grey pants, since this would be his uniform. Delta hadn't put much thought yet into what its male flight attendants would wear; the final instructions for these first stewards included directions to a recommended store in Atlanta. As always, women's dress gets more attention than men's!

Training went well for Eugene, but when he was appointed to the Houston base, he noticed a pattern in how Operations always called him late to report to a flight. They were supposed to provide at least four hours' notice, but he almost never got that much time. He always made it (sometimes he never actually left the airport if he knew he'd be on regular duty the next day), but it was always close. If he hadn't made it, missing flights would have counted as "no shows" on his record, and if he'd accumulated enough, they would have been grounds for termination. Of course, they were always apologetic when this happened, but it occurred so often that he was certain that it was directed at him, though he didn't know if it was because he was black, a black man, or both. Sure enough, about twenty years later, one of the people in Operations who had been instrumental in making his early years so turbulent apologized to Eugene.

Just as we had experienced ten years earlier in Miami, buildings convenient to the airport suddenly didn't have anything left when a black man showed up, asking to rent. He finally found an apartment near the airport and settled in for this new career.

He also found a cold welcome in other cities. On one of his layovers in New York, the crew all walked into the hotel and signed in for their pre-arranged reservations. Eugene was the last to sign in, and the clerk told him that they simply didn't have any rooms left (even though Delta always arranged reservations beforehand so that there would be enough rooms) and that he'd have to find another hotel. The rest of the crew had already gone up to their rooms and, in any case, the crew culture wasn't quite close-knit enough to be able to ask to share a room.

He found a cab that had been sitting outside the hotel and asked to go to the nearest hotel. Hotel after hotel, when he got to the desk to ask for a room, they were all full. He finally decided that he stood no chance of getting a room, so he told the cab driver to take him to the original hotel. A crew member greeted him, saying he was early for pickup and asking him if he couldn't sleep. "No, I'm not early. I haven't been to bed yet. I've been riding around all night looking for a room."

Later that year, Eugene was joined by three others: Art Lane, Fred Kelly, Steve Daniels, and Anthony Robinson. Now that we had male and female flight attendants, there were plenty of romances and sometimes things got complicated, to say the least. Ken was not only handsome but suave beyond the telling. (We called him Ken once somebody noticed that he resembled the Ken doll, of Barbie and Ken fame.) He needed every ounce of that suavity during a flight where, as it happened, two of his girlfriends were attendants on the same flight. He almost managed to keep his juggling act and keep the two of them from realizing that he had another girlfriend on the flight, but by the end of the flight, he wasn't dating either of them anymore. However, despite whatever the ladies might have wanted to say to him or to each other, the passengers didn't notice a thing, although everybody else on the flight crew went home, snickering. Later, Ken married a gorgeous blue-eyed blonde flight attendant, and, of course we all called her Barbie.

THE POSITION OF FLIGHT ATTENDANT IN CHARGE was granted to the most senior person on a flight, provided that she (or later he) had gone through supervisory training. We knew then that it was only a matter of time until there would be a black flight attendant in charge. On the management side, promotions were more or less at management's discretion. It wasn't until 1974 that Elaine McKinney became the first black flight attendant supervisor in management in Chicago.

The majority of the flight attendants got along and worked very well together. Many of us have remained close friends to this day. However, sometimes there was tension between the flight attendants and the rest of the crew, possibly because the African American flight attendants were integrated before the cockpit was. On one occasion a Chicago-based pilot accused the mostly black crew (seven black, one white) of drinking while on the flight. His evidence? They were having too much fun, laughing and joking, so obviously they had to have been drinking. He called the base and asked that management meet and question the crew. Management found that no one had been drinking. The matter was dropped. We always had a great time going to work; we thoroughly enjoyed what we were doing and saw it as having great fun with our friends.

Back in those days, we were allowed to give passengers complimentary miniature bottles of liquor to take with them from first class, especially if they were celebrating a special occasion or even simply asked for them. On one flight, I was the only black flight attendant on the plane. One other member of the crew took an immediate dislike to me and ostentatiously ignored me when I introduced myself. After the flight, she witnessed me putting a few bottles in a bag to hand to a passenger and told the only other flight attendant on board, Debbie Phillips, that she thought I was stealing liquor.

I had flown several times before with Debbie, and she was one of my closest friends, so that attendant must have gotten the shock of her life when Debbie quickly informed her that she knew I would never steal liquor and that she didn't appreciate the accusation. Debbie then told me what had happened, adding that she was certain that it was because of my race, based on some other remarks that the accuser had added. Debbie wanted to close the matter there, but I didn't feel it would be closed until I had addressed my accuser personally.

The next chance I got, I asked the girl to meet me down in the galley because I had something to discuss with her. When we were alone in the galley, I asked why she had accused me of theft. She said that she assumed I had been stealing because I was putting the liquor bottles into a bag. I told her that wasn't evidence of anything and warned her that coming onto a new base and accusing her colleagues of theft was a way to make enemies—or, as I put it, get her ass kicked—and that she'd made a mistake in assuming that Debbie would be on her side. She burst into tears. I told her that tears wouldn't work on me and that she wasn't getting out of anything by turning on the waterworks.

I ended by asking her if she was positive that this was over, saying that we could have a supervisor meet the flight if she didn't agree that it was resolved. She apologized and said that it was over. To cover myself, I met with my supervisor to tell her what happened, so I could have my side of the story on record. I never heard anything about it afterward, especially after my accuser transferred out of the base.

It wasn't a time for sour expressions. We were happy and young, seeing the world and meeting great people, and we were living the American dream. We handled most disagreements at our home base, and most supervisors knew us and our integrity personally. Most incidents, like this one, were resolved with no repercussions after individual interviews.

CHAPTER EIGHT:

The People We Encountered

P ART OF THE GLAMOUR OF BEING A FLIGHT ATTENDANT was meeting famous political figures, sports players, and other celebrities. Before the days of private jets, virtually every public figure flew commercial. This was also in the time when tickets were very expensive for everybody, so flying commercial was still very exclusive, especially in first class.

In most cases, the celebrities were very friendly and approachable, perhaps because, after all, the flight attendants can either provide or withhold the liquor. We stewardesses had our own glamour then, and so none of them seemed to feel as though chatting with us was mingling too much with the common herd. There were more than a few who assumed that the only reason that attractive women would want to be stewardesses was to meet prospective husbands, boyfriends, or to have one-night stands. In some cases, this was even true—it was almost like a high-end dating service in the sky, where rich men could meet glamorous and beautiful women. As a dating service, it was pretty successful.

Our new lives had dangers as well as excitement, lots of eligible singles, and career fulfillment. Drinking was one issue, but we had very strict rules about not drinking alcohol when we were on call or in the air. However, drinking did go on when people were off duty. On one of our longer layovers (ten hours or more), certain floors or rooms in hotels that Delta had contracted with were reserved only for crew members. In one of our regular layover hotels in Santa Monica, it was common to play a slightly more mature version of an Easter egg hunt and find miniature bottles of alcohol (the same ones that we served during flights) hidden in ingenious locations such as curtain hems, behind the curtains on the window sill, or on the floor behind furniture or any other object that hid them from sight. We always wondered why the cleaning staff never removed the bottles, or maybe it was because they never cleaned behind the curtains.

The honor code among the flight attendants said that you couldn't drink from them unless you replaced the contents and put it back where you found it. It was actually legal to drink during layover as long as you had eight hours or more until your next flight, but removing the liquor bottles from the airplane was strictly forbidden. Sometimes I wondered if people took them for the sake of breaking the rule rather than the value of the liquor. Most of that drinking was fairly moderate, although there were incidents with intoxicated pilots or flight crew members.

As drugs became more widely available in the 1960s and were considered less shameful than before, many flight attendants gave in to the temptations that drugs offered. Marijuana was the most popular in the 1960s, but the harder drugs were around, too.

☙〇❧

FLIGHT ATTENDANT, BRENDA HOGAN WHITE, had a reputation as a popular colleague and for her dating escapades. One famous story was how she was dating comedian Redd Foxx, star of the *Sanford and Son* show. One of the stories told how he would send a limo to pick her up from the airport on her layover. While people were deplaning, she would go into the plane bathroom, wearing her uniform, and make a grand exit several minutes later, wearing her after-five dress and full-length mink coat. We never could figure out how she did it in that bathroom, since they were just as tiny and cramped then as they are now, but she emerged looking like she'd come out of a Hollywood star's dressing room. Redd Foxx was close friends with Flip Wilson, another comedian, famous for his female impersonation of a character named Geraldine. Rumor said that Brenda was dating him, too, and once they both found out they were dating her, it caused a rift in their friendship.

The first time I met Brenda, I was studying in my room. Another student, Adrian, came by and said, "Hey, Casey, if you can take a break from studying, come to the lobby so you can meet my girlfriend. She's been flying for a few years, and she's coming over with one of the Atlanta Falcons." I happily agreed, excited to meet my first full-fledged black stewardess and her professional football player date. It definitely confirmed that I was going to love this new life.

Brenda walked in, wearing a black jumpsuit, long hair, and red nails, and a huge smoky topaz ring. (I tried to emulate her years later and bought the largest ring I could find with one of my first real paychecks, just because she had looked so cool with hers—and it is my birthstone.) She could have been Josephine Baker's twin sister, with the same beauty and glamour and daring style, and here we were chatting while I was training for the same career as hers.

But living the fast life took its toll on her. She took any number of risks and often the consequences caught up with her. She had various brushes with the law and once was even arrested for driving the getaway car during a robbery, though she claimed she didn't know what her friends were planning to do when they got out of the car. On February 15, 1977, she left her mother's house in Houston and seemed to disappear off the face of the earth. Later, her body was found on the side of a California expressway, and, because there was no way of identifying her, she was buried in an unmarked grave in Los Angeles.

The autopsy determined that she had died of a drug overdose. It wasn't until more than twenty years later that her sister heard of a new DNA testing facility in Dallas, which had solved missing persons' cases, including another person who had been missing for decades. Her family sent hair from one of Brenda's hairbrushes to the facility. They identified her as the person in that unmarked grave, so her family at least knew what had happened and could bury her remains near her home, with a proper service.

∽o∾

THAT WAS A PERIL OF LIVING LIFE IN THE FAST LANE, but we faced many that were specific to flying. Thanks to advanced equipment and crew training, there are very few crashes or catastrophic equipment failures, but we always had to be prepared for the worst.

Airplanes get struck by lightning fairly regularly, but the planes are designed to withstand even several strikes. However, it's still quite the experience. During one flight, we flew into a storm, and, because of the turbulence, the pilot instructed the attendants to take our seats and strap ourselves in. It was a night flight and we had dimmed the lights. Suddenly, there was a loud bang, and the inside of the plane lit up like something out of a science fiction movie as white and blue static electricity rolled from the front of the plane to the rear. We knew what it was and that the plane was equipped for it. In its own way, it was an exciting visual display, but we were glad that the few passengers who were awake and looking into the aisle didn't panic.

While motion pictures and television movies show widespread passenger panic during emergencies, it really doesn't happen that often in real life. Of course, every flight attendant has stories about passengers with a phobia about flying or claustrophobia, but group panic is very rare. We like to think that part of their calm is in knowing that they are in the hands of professionals and that the flight attendants, as the face of the flight crew, share responsibility.

Once on a flight from Miami to Atlanta, we were in the middle of beverage service when the captain summoned the head flight attendant via our onboard telephone system to come to the cockpit. He informed her that the plane, a DC-9, had lost power in one of the two engines, and we needed to prepare for an emergency landing. We knew that the DC-9 could continue flying at the current altitude but that the landing could be difficult. If anything went wrong with the descent, he might not have enough power to pull back up sharply. In other words, he had to get the landing right because there was no margin for error or if anything unforeseen happened.

This sounds rather horrifying, but, in reality, we knew that the situation was under control. Pilots train for situations like this one and worse in the simulators, and ground crews are ready for these situations, too.

We had more than forty-five minutes to prepare for landing, briefing all of the passengers to place any sharp objects deep in the seat pockets, check that their seatbelts were securely fastened, and (since this was in the days before carry on infant seats) to hold any children securely in their laps. We also told them how to assume crash position (bend over and grab their ankles to minimize the chance of being thrown about or of whiplash, and to stay low and buckled until instructed that the plane had come to a complete and final stop). The ground personnel and control tower were preparing in the meantime, making sure that we would have as good an approach as possible to a clear runway.

The equipment lights in the cockpit showed that as we approached, the landing gear was properly lowered and locked, and the descent was absolutely normal. We gave the signal to the passengers to assume the bracing position. The landing was absolutely uneventful. We had expected it to be, but still we were all very relieved, as were the passengers. They calmly gathered their belongings and as they got off the plane, the pilot thanked each and every one of them for maintaining calm and helping to make it a safe landing. They, of course, thanked him for making the safe landing possible. The only aftermath was another set of paperwork to be filled out. As much as we disliked the paperwork, we knew that it was part of helping to make sure the next landing like this one would be just as safe, so we didn't even begrudge it too much. (Just the usual amount)

ᚺᛟᚺ

IN THOSE DAYS, ALMOST ALL AIRLINE HIJACKINGS involved people wanting to go to Cuba. A huge wave of hijackings started in 1968, when there were two or three almost every month. It had mostly died down by 1973, due to Nixon's ordering the presence of air marshals (armed federal agents) in 1970, the installation of metal detectors in airports, and to a treaty between the United States and Cuba, agreeing to prosecute hijackers. Even with all that, there were still one or two hijackings each year throughout the 1990s. Some hijackers were Cuban nationals, others were Americans, and still others were foreign nationals. The most common motives were making a political statement and finding a way around the travel restrictions between the United States and Cuba.

Almost none of them wanted to hurt anybody, and so the FAA training emphasized cooperating with the hijackers and specifically forbade "heroic measures." If there was a hijacking, the crew was to keep the other passengers calm, relay hijacker demands to the authorities, and take the hijackers to their destinations. As hijackings became more common, there were even standard procedures for returning the planes and other passengers.

It seems odd today, but back then, hijackings seemed so innocuous that some comedians even made "Take me to Cuba" the punch line of various jokes or skits. Of course, we still had to be cautious, since some of the hijackers really did have the bombs that they claimed to have or had real guns, and others were mentally unstable, but overall, to us it was more like an inconvenient reroute than the truly terrifying situation that hijackings became after 9/11.

Back then, many of the hijackers seemed to perceive black flight attendants as being potentially more sympathetic and willing to act as mediators. This was never a focus of the training, but several African Americans who were part of flight crews on hijacked planes reported that the hijackers seemed to call upon them more often to act as mediators and to carry their communications.

Because there were so few incidents, airport security was almost non-existent then, too. There were police at the airport to take care of disorderly people, but that was about all. There were no metal detectors, and anybody could come into the boarding area to drop off or to meet a passenger.

We were responsible, however, for keeping an eye on people that we thought might be trouble, and we received instructions on profiling suspicious behaviors.

In almost all cases, though, these were false alarms. For example, I was waiting in the boarding area for the plane to be cleared so we could board, and I noticed a passenger who was sweating and pacing back and forth between the window and the seating area, anxiously looking at the plane. I alerted the boarding agent, who said that she had already called for security. The airport security came, took him off to a private area, and did some low-key questioning. It turned out that he was only a nervous flyer and a new member of what we called the White Knuckle Club.

⌘

DESPITE ALL THAT, HIJACKINGS WERE STILL SCARY for everybody, those on the plane and those on the ground, who knew they might not find out what was going on until it was over. One that sticks in my mind is a 1980 flight when Sarah Qualls and eight other members of the flight crew, along with fifty-three passengers, were flying from Chicago to New York on the L1011 Tri-Star, one of the safest and most technologically advanced aircrafts of its time, known as the Rolls Royce of the sky.

During this night flight, a passenger approached one of the flight attendants, saying that he was hijacking the aircraft and wanted his demands delivered to the news media. He gave her a note with his demands that included payment of $14 million to Ayatollah Khomeini, then the spiritual leader (and for all practical purposes, the supreme leader) of Iran, which then was holding fifty-two Americans captive in the U.S. embassy. He also wanted money and gold delivered to the Nation of Islam. The hijacker's sister had died, he wanted to scatter her ashes on Iranian soil, and he ordered the plane to go to Iran. He also said that blacks weren't "being treated fairly and were oppressed in America" and should "go to another country where we would be treated fairly."

The flight crew advised him that the aircraft wasn't equipped to go to Iran; they didn't even think he was very serious until they saw his gun. The flight attendant had informed Sarah, the on-board leader, that a passenger had told them he wanted to go to Iran. As Sarah approached the hijacker, she asked him again about his demands, which he repeated. She called the cockpit to relay his demands, and he then said that he had put a bomb on board. A passenger with a gun is already a serious threat, but one with a bomb is an entirely different emergency. The hijacker next demanded access to the cockpit.

The captain opened the cockpit door and explained that the plane wasn't equipped for international flights. While this was true, the pilot was also following established procedure to delay matters as long as possible, while appearing to comply with the hijacker's demands. The pilot transmitted all of the passenger's demands to Delta, taking as long as he could without angering the hijacker, and Delta did the same in sending its responses. The purpose of this was to give the authorities time to learn as much as they could and do what they could to protect the passengers and crew, and also to make the hijacker more willing to negotiate. Most hijackers then were amateurs and frequently more nervous than their hostages. Being taken seriously and given that taste of power would help them to calm down and keep them from doing anything rash that they might do if they felt rushed.

The hijacker also ordered that the male and female passengers separate. He wanted the women to move to the back of the cabin, and the men to come closer to the front, where he could keep a closer eye on them. All of the flight crew except Fred Kelly were women, and so Sarah asked whether Fred should join the male passengers or whether he could stay with the crew and work. The hijacker looked

Fred up and down and noticed that he was only very slightly built, not that he had a dancer's muscles, and said with a disparaging smirk, "I don't care where *he* goes." Big mistake.

These prolonged communications and negotiations worked as planned, and the hijacker finally agreed that Cuba would be acceptable. Sarah returned to the cabin and announced to the passengers that a passenger had requested the crew that they divert to another destination. This message, put in a way to cause as little alarm as possible, told the passengers that the flight was being hijacked. The second part of this announcement was for Sarah and the other flight attendants to direct the passengers to the information card, located in the seat pocket directly in front of each passenger, which explains the evacuation procedures and the emergency exits. This was to prepare passengers for the possibility of running out of fuel over water, since they were flying to Cuba. Considering the situation, the passengers remained relatively calm, knowing the odds were that the situation would end without violence.

George, one of the regulars on this Chicago to New York route, was a Wells Fargo currency courier. No one ever knew how much currency, but it was enough to justify his carrying it in person and being armed. He was authorized to carry a gun on the plane. He told Sarah that he was ready and willing to shoot and was perfectly placed for a quick, direct shot. This kind of speedy solution might have seemed like a gift right from God, sent to save all of those lives. Instead, while the crew was relieved to know that he was armed and in position, they told him to wait and be ready to receive further instructions from the captain or the company.

If the hijacker was alone, it would have been a viable solution, but if he had hidden accomplices, it would doubtless have led to a bloodbath. In addition, if the plan failed, the hijacker might have detonated a bomb (the crew still had no idea whether or not his threat was real) or otherwise retaliated violently, taking more lives, possibly all the lives on the plane.

Gunshots could have caused a deadly panic, and if shots hit the plane body and caused structural damage, that could have led to rapid decompression. One single bullet hole can't cause the kind of rapid decompression that sucks people out, but if there's a bigger hole, like the kind that even a small bomb can create in a window, or if a window were compromised by enough bullets hitting the right places, people could get sucked out.

For all of these reasons, they didn't want to take the risk unless they had absolutely no other choice. In addition, while the money was their smallest concern, compared to the safety of the passengers, crew, or even any ships below or planes nearby, they didn't want the hijacker or accomplices searching George and getting the money.

The thing about this kind of experience is that no matter how much training and practice scenarios emulating potentially dangerous situations we may encounter, nothing can prepare us completely for when it happens in real life. People who might be fearless for their own safety also can react very differently when they're responsible for the safety of others. Sarah was already shaken when the hijacker told her he had a gun and made his demands. When he later showed her the gun, she realized that he was at the very least telling the truth about being armed; she was even more horrified.

In a purely mechanical emergency, she would have explained the special procedures and given instructions to passengers about what to do in case of a water landing. These instructions were lengthy and detailed: what equipment the passengers had to take from their seats; how to properly stow all personal items rather than try to take them with them; why it is important to put away beverage glasses, high heeled shoes, and other potentially sharp items that could puncture life rafts; how to put on a life vest and properly inflate it at the right time (inflating them too soon could make it difficult or even impossible to evacuate quickly and safely); and how to put vests on infants.

Sarah decided it best to ask another flight attendant to make the announcements, so she could deal more effectively with the hijacker. The possibility of a water landing was yet another reason not to take direct action against the hijacker; while most water landings don't result in serious injuries or deaths, the risk is definitely there.

When the diverted plane landed in Cuba, they stayed on the ground for about fifteen hours. Gail Bibb, a flight attendant who spoke Spanish, interpreted the hijacker's demands to the Cuban authorities. One of the hijacker's demands was that Gil Noble, a reporter from New York, fly in from New York and act as his spokesperson.

Fred Kelly pulled Sarah aside and said "Sarah, I think we need to be proactive and think of an escape plan. He doesn't seem to want to hurt us. His ass just wants to go to Iran. Why don't we deploy the evacuation slides in the back cabin and leave his ass on the aircraft by himself?"

Sarah answered, "I think we need not to do anything crazy, but I agree we need to think of an escape plan." While she coordinated a plan with the captain, Fred and the other crew members put their heads together and fine-tuned his original plan.

The lower galley is the belly of the aircraft where the food and beverages are stored, accessed by lifts. They'd slowly move the passengers from their seats in the tourist cabin into the lifts that would take them to the lower galley area. Fred would be the first person out and would inform the Cubans that an escape was in progress. The challenge in that plan was that the Cubans knew the hijacker was a Black Muslim and might well shoot Fred, also a black man, on sight. Fred decided that the best approach would be to dangle his legs slowly out the lower galley door. He hoped this non-threatening gesture would alert the authorities that he was exiting in a peaceful manner. In addition, he'd tie a white napkin to his leg as an improvised surrender flag.

Ironically, the one Iranian passenger on board was afraid to exit on Cuban soil, thinking that the Cubans might decide that he was an accomplice or otherwise involved. The crew eventually persuaded him to exit the aircraft.

To make the evacuation plan more realistic and give the flight attendants that were involved time to execute the escape, the captain made an announcement that the front door would be opened to allow food to be brought on board for the passengers. This also meant that some flight attendants had to stay on board to distract the hijacker from realizing that passengers were being evacuated. From the hijacker's perspective in the front of the plane, he couldn't get a full view of the tourist cabin passenger seats, but he could see the flight attendants standing in the aisles as they pretended to serve passengers in the rapidly emptying seats. Every now and again, he'd glance back and be reassured that the flight attendants appeared to be acting normally.

It wasn't until the last passengers and the crew were gone that he took a longer, closer look, and realized that the plane was empty. Panic-stricken, he demanded to speak to the captain and renegotiate his demands. The engineer talked to him, but by then, the hijacker was so deflated that he didn't seem a threat any more. The engineer finally decided to open the front door, allowing the Cuban police to come on board and apprehend the hijacker. Everything had ended without bloodshed.

After the hours in the plane and hours of interrogation from the Cuban authorities, the crew and passengers, including the Iranian passenger, were allowed to fly to Miami. There, the FBI debriefed the crew and finally allowed them to fly back to their home base, Chicago. Believe it or not, most of the crew members reported back to work four days after this ordeal.

The hijacker was jailed in Cuba, but when Cuba started packing its criminals on boats and sending them to America, he was among them. He turned himself into U.S. authorities, and during the trial, it emerged that he was the son of a judge in New York and had robbed a bank with his first wife. He was sentenced to forty years in prison.

In the early days of commercial flight, the best way to minimize violence or deaths during hijackings was to comply with hijacker demands, or at least appear to comply. But after 9/11, the emphasis switched to heavy airport security and on never letting hijackers get near the cockpit. We'll take a closer look at those consequences in a later chapter.

CHAPTER NINE:

It's a New Day

IN 1978 THE AIRLINE DEREGULATION ACT OF 1978 changed flying and travel in general for airlines and passengers both. While it didn't change government control over safety or the FAA, it removed all government control over prices, routes, and the formation of new airlines. For the general public, this meant far more routes, a far greater choice of airlines, and a tremendous decrease in the price of airline tickets. Between 1976 and 1990, for example, in real dollars (that is, adjusted for inflation), the typical fare dropped by about 30 percent.

A number of small airlines came and went, or emerged and were swallowed up by bigger airlines. Unionized airlines had occasional serious labor issues over changes in routes, mergers and related changes, and so on, but since Delta was financially stable, we didn't worry about losing our jobs or being taken over, and Delta was one of the few airlines then that didn't have a flight attendants union.

We also were serving a whole new group of passengers who had never flown before and weren't sure what to expect. Several thought that flight attendants were like waitresses and tried to tip us. Delta was firm that flight attendants are not like waitresses, and the official policy required us to turn down tips. That said, sometimes somebody gave us big tips, including a few who tipped their flight attendant $100 (today almost $450), and we didn't always remember to turn those down. Those flights ended with us happily dividing the loot.

In the days before widespread private or corporate jets, coach passengers came within fairly close confines with the rich and famous, and we had to learn how to protect famous passengers' privacy by keeping people moving through first class. Fortunately, there weren't any incidents where people had to be asked more than once to move on. (It probably helped that this was before camera phones were invented.)

∽o∾

EUGENE HARMOND WAS SO PERSONABLE that he could make friends with anybody. On a layover in Las Vegas in the 1980s, Eugene ran into Patricia while he was passing through the lobby area of the hotel on his way to his room. He stopped to say hello. She confided, "Well, I'm a little disappointed because the other stewardesses on the flight had talked about doing this and that on the layover and invited me. I've been down here waiting, and I think I've been stood up. I figured I might as well see if I can find a good restaurant and have dinner."

He answered, "Oh, I'm sorry, Patricia. I have a buddy in town tonight doing a show. Do you want to go? It's Bill Cosby." Even though this was long before *The Cosby Show* made him a global household name, he was already one of the most famous comedians in the United States. Naturally, this brightened her up right away, and they agreed to meet at 5:00. As he approached her in the lobby, he said, "Bill told us to come on over to the Hilton and meet him for dinner before the show. Is that okay with you?"

Patricia naturally agreed happily and when they got to the Hilton, Eugene called Bill Cosby on the house phone and arranged to meet in the main restaurant. During a great dinner and wonderfully funny conversion, Cosby invited them to meet him in his dressing room backstage just before the show.

Patricia had always admired him as a very talented comedian and was impressed by how friendly and genuine he appeared to be. He handed Eugene two front-row seats and said he hoped they enjoyed the show, which they certainly did.

Eugene explained that he'd made friends with Cosby after they met on several flights where Eugene was serving first class. They struck up conversations that led to a genuine friendship. Cosby gave Eugene his number and invited him to call any time he was in Las Vegas and come to his show. Needless to say, Patricia didn't have any regrets about how the evening turned out.

Eugene bore a remarkable resemblance to Smokey Robinson, and once when I mentioned it to him, he leaned back in his chair and told me the story about his encounter with his double.

Eugene and a lady friend were hanging out in Las Vegas. His friend was a VIP at one of the casinos, and one of her perks that evening was front-row seating for a Smokey Robinson show. When Smokey Robinson saw them in seats, he invited them backstage. In another coincidence, Smokey had a picture in his dressing room of him posing with a horse. Only a month earlier, Eugene had a picture taken in almost exactly the same pose. Not the same horse, though.

❧⬥❧

ANOTHER CHANGE WAS THAT TOWARD THE END OF THE 1980S, the government required Delta and the other major airlines to implement mandatory random drug and alcohol testing for its flight crews. There was a culture of social drinking on layovers, and part of this was the combined stress and "nobody from home can see me" effect. This was social drinking, though, and we knew that we had to abstain from drinking a certain number of hours before we might be called for duty.

Just like in any profession, there were a few people who had drinking problems that affected their job performances, though usually this showed up in overuse of sick days. We always had more sick days than most companies gave their employees, because we were exposed to so many more colds and flu than most other people and because Delta knew that a sniffling flight attendant or one who just looked and sounded under the weather didn't make passengers happy. So, unless somebody had a serious illness or condition that management would already know about, using up all one's sick days would raise a red flag with the company.

Flight attendants were given a grace period to go to management without any repercussions and admit if they had a drug or alcohol problem. As long as they went to counseling, paid for by management, they wouldn't lose their jobs. Many asked for help but others didn't. They didn't want to quit or didn't believe that they could, so they planned to try to outsmart the tests. One flight attendant told me that her crack habit was so strong that she would stop in the middle of a meal service, leaving the other attendant to finish service unassisted, and go back to the restroom, deactivate the smoke detector, and light up her crack pipe. She and others later failed the random drug tests and were fired. Fortunately, there were very few incidents like these.

The 1980s was also the decade when everything started to change for the LGBT community in the United States. AIDS spread widely in the gay community and during the early days, was mistakenly considered "the gay disease" or "gay cancer." It's hard to convey today just what it was like then, when the diagnosis of HIV/AIDS meant that somebody might have only a few months left to live. We lost many good friends and colleagues during those years.

CHAPTER TEN:

Tragedies

IN 1988, WE HAD A TERRIBLE SHOCK when we lost another one of our first stars in the sky. Brenda Hogan died after she left Delta, but Brenda Louis McCullough Wheeler was killed in a terrible act of senseless violence while she still worked for Delta. In losing her, we lost not only a friend and colleague, but also one of the pioneers. Those of us who came after her were aware of the debt that we owed to her, since our predecessors were the first ones to desegregate the skies and not only bore the brunt of prejudice but also were the ones who disarmed it.

Brenda was from Memphis and had flown for twenty-two years when she was murdered at the age of forty-two in Atlanta. She had gone out to purchase a white Christmas tree—one of the new fashions—and when she returned home, she walked in on a burglary in progress. They tied her up and battered her to death with a hammer before fleeing the scene. Her ten-year-old son found her. He tried to wake her up by shaking her and then called his teacher, who called the police for him. The police found the killers because she had marked the possessions that they had stolen, and the pawn shop noticed the markings and reported them.

Brenda had a great personality and an infectious laugh. She was petite in physical stature but her demeanor commanded respect. Attractive, professional, and efficient, she seemed to epitomize the contemporary stewardess. She lived her life to the fullest and took advantage of the opportunity to live the glamorous life. She socialized with some of Atlanta's elite, and her young children often traveled with her, which then was a rare privilege.

The last time I saw her she was a load factor, which is what we called the extra flight attendants when a flight was heavy or we needed to have a specific number of attendants on board to comply with FAA standards. She'd said that she wasn't feeling well but was going to do her best. After we had completed the service and there wasn't anything that we needed her to do, we sent her down to the lower galley to rest, and I checked on her a while later. She was in the jump seat with her head down on the tray table like a student sleeping on a desk at school. I asked her if she was all right and if there was anything I could do for her. She smiled and said, "Girl, I'm not sick, I'm hung over. I partied hard all night in Vegas, and I just need to get some sleep." I laughed and gave her a pillow and blanket and that was the last time I saw her.

∽o∾

SOMETIMES THINGS HAPPENED THAT SEEMED RIGHT OUT OF THE MOVIES. One day in the mid-1980s, my flight from Atlanta to Chicago started out as any other trip. After the service had been completed, all service items were picked up, and the aircraft was secured ready for landing. Janet Jones and I were sitting at 3L and 3R, the right and left flight attendant foldout seats.

Upon landing, the passenger sitting in the middle seat at the bulkhead fell out of his seat. Engines were in the reversed position, which meant that according to FAA regulations, we couldn't get up unless the whole airplane was in danger, so we had to wait until the plane slowed down. Janet and I approached him at the same time, shook him, and yelled, "Are you okay?" There was no response. We checked for a pulse and breathing and paged for medical assistance. Just as the help came, he made a loud noise, like a snore, and I noticed a bottle of nitroglycerine, which heart patients use. I asked him if he was in pain and if he had chest pains, and he said no each time. I asked if they were his pills, and he said they were. When I asked how many he had taken, he became visibly afraid and answered that he had tried to kill himself because "They were trying to kill me." I was absolutely baffled and unable to think of what else to ask, I asked, "Who?"

He pointed to the back of the plane to where two young men and a young woman were standing and watching. Their eyes were fixed on him, and they were taking down their luggage in very slow motion. I could tell that they were trying to determine what he was saying to us and how we were reacting. A quick look at the other attendants and the doctor confirmed that none of them believed him, either, despite the observers' behavior.

Everybody else deplaned, except for the sick passenger and the three passengers who were stalling as they kept their eyes on us. The passenger was finally able to sit up and was more coherent as the pilot talked to him and asked to see his ticket, which was a one-way ticket from Miami to Chicago, paid for in cash. He was still sweating and afraid.

The pilot asked an agent to direct him to baggage claim, but we noticed the other three passengers still lingering, pretending to be doing something and watching us talk to him. At first, we thought that his claims that somebody was trying to kill him were either delusions or a disturbed individual's desire for attention, but seeing those other three passengers lingering and watching gave us all second thoughts. Could this scenario actually be true?

In any case, whether his story was true or not, the procedure was the same. The agent continued to escort him down to baggage claim. The moment he was downstairs, he jumped onto the conveyer belt, trying to run away. Airport security apprehended him and arrested him for entering a secured area, taking him to a police station and jailing him overnight.

A friend of mine who had watched the news that night called me the next morning to tell me the news. It turned out that the passenger was telling the truth.

Earlier that day, in a courtroom in downtown Chicago, that very passenger had given a small piece of paper with a phone number written on it to a guard and asked him to call the number and tell whoever answered the phone what had happened to him. As the guard put the note away, the man grabbed the guard's gun and fatally shot himself in the head, in front of the crowded courtroom.

Another friend of mine, who had been on that flight, called me later when the final details emerged. According to the accounts, the passenger was a drug dealer who had tried to take more than his agreed-upon share of the proceeds. His colleagues found out and when he saw other members of the group on the plane, he decided it was better to kill himself rather than wait for them to do it. When taking the nitroglycerine failed, being in police custody protected him until he was in the courtroom, when he finally killed himself to avoid a worse punishment.

∽∽o∽∽

DELTA CONTINUED TO EXPAND ITS BLACK FLIGHT CREWS, and by the 1980s, most of the pioneers had enough seniority to get the really choice assignments on the best planes, including that L1011, the Rolls Royce of the skies. All of us having seniority together meant that as often as not, the flight crew might be half or all African American. When this happened and we were all in boarding position, from the pilot to the ten flight attendants, we watched the passengers react to the realization that they were being transported and served by an all-black crew. Even in Chicago, with its large black population, this shocked many of our passengers, and we could sometimes see people notice this and say something to their traveling companions. However, we never heard a word of protest and took our places proudly.

Chicago base was a close and unique bunch of flight attendants and always a joy to work with. We all seemed to have grown up together and have supported each other through marriages, divorce or just difficult times and have maintained our friendships to this day. When we see each other, it doesn't take long to exchange updates, wish each other well, and look forward to seeing each other again.

CHAPTER ELEVEN:

Going International

I N 1991 DELTA TOOK OVER PAN AM, which had been one of the largest and most glamorous international airlines. Pan Am had the equivalent of the Ivy League of flight attendants; they had to speak at least two languages and were almost celebrities. In her 1987 book, *Femininity in Flight: A History of Flight Attendants*, Kathleen M. Barry quoted a black flight attendant as saying in a 1972 *New York Times* interview, "After all, next to being a movie star or beauty queen, no position or job so tenaciously heralds a woman's beauty and femininity." For me, this epitomized the image of the Pan Am flight attendants, as poised and beautiful as glamorous movie stars.

For us, this merger was tremendously exciting and presented great new opportunities, especially for those of us who had enough seniority to fly the international routes. Only a few of us had ever been overseas and thus a whole new world was opening up. We had had a few international flights, including ones to Seoul, Paris, and Frankfurt but only a few of these, and they were all out of the Atlanta, Portland (Oregon), or Cincinnati bases, so comparatively only a small number of us were able to fly internationally, perhaps 5 or 10 percent.

Not only was Delta flying to dozens of new countries it had never flown to before, we had more bases, including one in New York, and more of our bases flew internationally. For those of us with enough seniority, it meant that in one month, we could have a trip to two or more exciting places such as Ghana, Rome, Dublin, Istanbul, Athens, Bangkok, Moscow, and London.

I never flew on one of the African routes, but for many black flight attendants, seeing Ghana was a particularly moving experience. For most, it was the first glimpse of any African country or an African culture, outside of documentaries or books, and it was a thrill to see our motherland.

I transferred to New York to take advantage of these international opportunities and found it opened up a whole new world and new experiences. Some of these were pure hedonism, such as finding new restaurants or shops in exotic places, but others had their alarming moments.

∽ﻬ∾

DURING THE 1990S, MANY PARTS OF EUROPE were facing deep unrest. The Soviet Union collapsed, Germany reunified, there was tremendous ethnic violence in the former Yugoslavia, and, during the first part of the decade, the IRA was still active in Ireland and the UK.

On one of my first trips overseas—to Athens—we landed a distance from the terminal, expecting a bus to take us to the main terminal. Instead, we were met by the bus, a tank, and armed soldiers. The soldiers escorted our bus to the main terminal because of some unrest in the city. While we didn't see anything that suggested any kind of danger, seeing that tank unsettled us all.

On another layover in Athens, the streets were in turmoil because somebody on a motorcycle had just shot at a public official. Police and security forces rapidly lined the streets to control the crowds and protestors.

ONE MORNING IN APRIL 2001, I was getting dressed in my hotel room in Istanbul and listening to the CNN news channel when I heard a roaring sound outside the window. I went to investigate and saw several helicopters overhead but nothing else unusual. One of the reporters said that a small group had taken over a downtown hotel, but without any more information than that, I assumed that our crew wasn't in any danger.

I left the room and took the elevator to the first floor, where the first thing I saw was a lobby full of soldiers, machine guns at their sides, before I even saw the rest of the flight crew. One soldier approached me and looked at the captain to confirm that I was part of the crew and escorted me across the lobby to the rest of the crew. They told us that in addition to the hotel, an international airline crew had been taken hostage. Nobody knew the group's identity or demands.

We were given a police escort to the airport and arrived safely. The flight was calm, but it wasn't until we landed and could check the news again that we knew what had happened. A Turkish citizen of Chechen ancestry and a small group of other Chechen sympathizers had invaded the hotel and taken almost two hundred guests and staff hostage to protest Russia's policies in Chechnya. The situation lasted about twelve hours and ended peaceably; in fact, the ringleader apologized to the Turkish people for the inconvenience.

WHILE WE WERE NEVER DIRECTLY INVOLVED IN ANY OF THESE OVERSEAS CRISES, we had crises of our own. In the mid-1990s, Delta introduced a Critical Incident Response Program (CIRP) to its flight crews. This program helps crew members to cope with the aftermath of tragedies, including deaths on the job and plane crashes. I had just finished my training for this program in 1997 when such a tragedy struck.

When you look out the window of a plane on the tarmac, before the plane moves into position for takeoff or comes to the gate for landing, you'll see people with lights in their hands, guiding the pilot and communicating with the Air Traffic Control (ATC). Their job is to remove the auxiliary power units that connect to the communication units and to alert the pilot if there's anything obstructing the wings since the pilot doesn't have all of the plane's width in a clear line of vision. Because of this, they're called wing walkers, though this has nothing to do with stunts people walking on the wings of a plane in mid-flight.

Each wing walker is responsible for his or her own section of the takeoff or landing, and they make eye contact and signal to one another when their section is over and it's time for the next person to take charge of guiding the plane safely. The team members have to rely on one another, and this builds up real camaraderie and trust.

A friend and coworker, Debra Surrett, and I were deadheading (flying while not on duty) on a New York to Chicago flight, returning home from serving on a flight in Europe. We were all settled in our seats, and the door hadn't yet closed. It was past departure time when the pilot announced that there had been an incident and there would be a slight delay. I went into the galley, since the flight attendants were friends of mine, said hello and asked if there was any further information on the delay. They told me, very quietly, that they had heard that one of the ramp workers had been struck by a plane. They didn't know exactly what had happened, but we knew it had to be serious.

I told the head flight attendant to tell the captain that I was a certified CIRP member. She did, and he contacted the company to confirm that I was indeed who I said I was and was fully qualified. He was able to see, from his seat, that things were very bad, so he came out, briefed me on what he knew so far, and asked me for assistance.

A wing walker had been hit and run over by the tire of the nose gear on a 767 plane, bound for Nice, France, that was exiting the gate. The pilot couldn't see him and hadn't seen the actual moment, but he could see people converging on the spot and bodies fallen on the tarmac. His first thought, based on the bodies, was that there was a sniper somewhere. He radioed the tower, and they told him that a wing walker had been hit and dismembered. The bodies he saw were ramp crew members who had come over to see what happened and passed out at the sight.

One of the difficult decisions that the airport staff had to make was how to remove the body parts from the tire wheel well. Moving the aircraft would continue to mangle his body, a prospect which so troubled everybody that they decided instead to try to jack up the wheel of the aircraft and remove him, piece by piece, as respectfully as possible.

I went back to collect my suitcase and tell Debra what had happened and that I wouldn't be flying back to Chicago with her. Debra offered to stay in New York to help me, and we left the plane to talk to the station manager. He set us up in a vacant office, so while she passed out beverages and tissues and prayed with those who wished to, I spent a few minutes myself in quiet prayer, asking God to help me to do no harm and to help and assist those in need. I was ready to fulfill my responsibility.

The first person who came into the private room that we had set up was the person most directly affected, the driver of the vehicle that pushes the plane back from the gate. He was very clearly in shock, tears running down his face, and his voice was shaking when he spoke so low that I had to strain to hear him. One of the first things we learned in our training was not to touch the colleagues that we are counseling, but I had to break that rule immediately. I took him in my arms, hugging him and patting his back as he kept repeating, "It wasn't my fault. I followed all the procedures" and "Not Wayne, not Wayne." We're also not supposed to comment on the situations or say anything that could be considered official, but I said what he most needed to hear, that it was an accident, that it wasn't his fault. I kept holding and reassuring him of that.

He indeed hadn't done anything wrong. Nobody can be sure exactly what happened, but it seemed as if Wayne was standing on the piece of metal that covers the tire. By a freak accident, his uniform pant leg got caught and pulled him down and under the wheel, and as the plane continued to move, severed him in half.

Over the next six hours, I saw members of the ramp crews and operations crews. Everybody was devastated not just by the loss of a colleague, but by the horrific nature of the accident. I learned more about the victim, including that he had gotten engaged just a few weeks before. Sometimes I waited for people to come to me; other times I went out to where people huddled, getting more information or just comforting one another. I even offered counseling to the New York City policemen who were still on the scene; of course, the police have their own providers for this, but as long as they were there and seemed so devastated, I had to offer. They accepted and talked through what they had seen. They were entirely professional, of course, and I knew that as New York policemen, they had certainly seen things just as horrifying or even worse, but still, this accident was so terrible that it took its toll on them, too, and talking helped.

After about eight hours, Debra and I were beyond exhaustion. We'd been on duty on the Rome to New York flight, and with that, the jet lag and time zone changes, we were already tired when we got on the plane to Chicago. I think it was adrenaline that gave us what we needed to get through those hours, and once the adrenaline was gone, we were ready to drop.

I filled out a tremendous amount of paperwork to send to Delta, which then assigned a professional psychologist to the cases. Some ground personnel, though, wanted to continue talking with me, so Delta flew me out to New York again. I was secretly relieved by this, since my time spent with the ground personnel there had truly formed a bond between us. My training had given me an excellent preparation for helping my colleagues, and our shared backgrounds with Delta and with flying made it easier for us to talk than it would have been for somebody outside the airline culture. So we needed one another then. In some cases, we remained in touch long after the accident, having formed a friendship as part of that bond.

After all of this was done, I myself, as part of my debriefing, had a session with the professional psychologist. While I hadn't seen the body, knowing the details and talking with the people who were so traumatized was a tremendous strain, but my training and the mutual support that we found helped me to process what had happened and continue to function as a flight attendant and in my daily life.

CHAPTER TWELVE:

Giving Back

WE ALSO CAME TOGETHER TO HELP ONE ANOTHER in our personal lives. In 1974 Jacqueline Jacquet-Williams, a flight attendant for Continental, founded Black Flight Attendants of America, Inc, with the mission of "serving the skies and serving the community." It was headquartered in California, so we weren't often able to participate in their events, but several of us joined to support it and show our solidarity. Many of us felt the need for a similar organization in Chicago.

While flight attendants could earn excellent money, enough for a very solid middle class income, this was dependent on how many hours they could fly. People with family obligations, especially single parents, had fewer opportunities to fly as many hours or to make as much money. One day, Valerie Costello, a single mother, and I were talking about how she was trying to go to school to pursue a career in dentistry and struggling to make enough money, especially since she wasn't able to find applicable scholarship opportunities.

After we talked for some time, I mentioned that thirty other Chicago-based African American flight attendants, mostly from Delta, and I had been trying to organize a group that would raise funds to help those in need. We hadn't gotten as far as targeting a specific cause, so I asked Valerie if it would be all right to take the idea of scholarships for single women to the group.

At the next meeting, we discussed Valerie and the idea of providing scholarships to women who were seeking assistance to pursue college or vocational education, and we agreed to make this our organization's purpose, with an emphasis on helping single mothers. We'd not only hand the recipients a $2000 scholarship check but also provide them with ongoing mentoring and encouragement.

Shelley Crump knew the internationally famous Ghanan American artist Samuel Akainyah, who had studied art at the School of the Art Institute of Chicago (SAIC) and received a master's degree in diplomacy and international law from the University of Chicago, and mentioned the group to him. He offered to design our logo and suggested that we name the organization to honor Yaa Asantewaa, (pronounced A-san-TE-WAA) a queen mother of the Edweso tribe of the Asante (Ashanti), now modern Ghana.

The name epitomized a woman of dexterity, intelligence, commitment, and courage. We incorporated it as a formal non-profit organization in May 1993 as our way of giving back to other African Americans and our community.

We appointed Valerie Costello president and Karla Brakett-Wiley vice-president. I was secretary and Loretta Mayes was treasurer. We also appointed Sarah Qualls, from the hijacking episode, as sergeant at arms. Wanda Wilson, who had been one of the flight attendants when a passenger died on board, and Jamie Young gathered the profiles of the potential recipients for the group.

Any minority woman, with connections to the airline industry or not, could apply simply by getting an application form from one of the members and describing how she and her family would benefit from the scholarship. Rather than using grade point averages or more traditional criteria, we looked for the applicants who had the strongest desire to improve their status through education and seemed the most capable of doing so.

In our first year, we raised enough monies from selling tickets to a formal dinner and raffle tickets for various prizes, including art and sculptures from a store in Greece where we had shopped frequently during our travels. Yanni, the store owner, gave us something each year. Individually, we committed to selling tickets for at least one table (ten people). As a result, that year we were able to award three scholarships.

While the scholarships were our primary cause, we also donated money to a home for mothers with disabilities and their children, donated money and volunteered to help feed the hungry through various Chicago churches and other organizations, and participated in career days at local high schools. One of our favorite moments was when Valerie went to a local church to offer a donation to their Christmas fund. The person in charge told Valerie she had just been in deep prayer asking for God to help them find a way to provide children in the congregation with Christmas presents, as so many were in families that couldn't afford gifts. Valerie asked how many boys and girls there were and their ages, and she passed this information on to us, so each of us bought toys for their Christmas.

At first, we didn't have the resources for publicity, so we simply spread the news through word of mouth. Later, I called *The Chicago Defender*, a weekly newspaper for African Americans, and asked them to publicize our fundraising events. They featured our work in the May 9, 1995 issue, including a photograph. The next year, on June 25, we were featured on the front page. Appearing in the same newspaper that Langston Hughes and Gwendolyn Brooks wrote for was a tremendous honor.

In October 1997, Asantewaa was listed in *Ebony* as a source for scholarships. This recognition meant a great deal to us because *Ebony*, founded in 1945 in Chicago by John H. Johnson, was and remains one of the first publications to celebrate African and African American achievements. Together with its sister publication, *Jet*, it has a circulation of 2.7 million, even in a time when magazines are disappearing left and right.

While our spirit was in the organization, our increasingly busy and varied schedules and lives didn't allow for the full commitment that it required. Flying different routes so often made it almost impossible for us to meet or to organize our fundraisers, so we disbanded the organization in 2002. As much as we loved flying, it took a toll on our personal lives and aspirations.

One of the reasons I was unable to participate as much as I would have liked was an in-flight injury in 2000. In my career, I didn't have that many crazy passengers to deal with, but this particular one was several years' worth of compressed crazy.

CHAPTER THIRTEEN:

Frustrations in the Sky

O N A FLIGHT FROM ROME TO NEW YORK'S JFK AIRPORT, I was the flight attendant in charge. My crew had complained to me several times that the couple sitting in business class seats 6A and B had been violently arguing, and the situation could possibly escalate. After we made it through the service, I was sitting on the jump seat when the passenger from 6B came up to me with his bloody right hand extended with a tooth rolling around in his palm. I asked, "What is that?" which seemed like a very reasonable question.

"Look what she's done to me. She's knocked out my tooth. I want you to move her, and I want her arrested once we land in New York."

I asked him to follow me back to where they were sitting. Once there, I said to him, "Sir, I'm going to separate you two. Will you please take seat 12A in the next section?" He gathered his belongings and proceeded to his new cabin and passenger seat.

I took the seat next to his girlfriend, a tall, slender brunette, and I said, "Hi, my name is Ms. Grant and I'm the flight attendant in charge. Your boyfriend said you knocked his tooth out. Is this true and if so, why?"

She answered, "I didn't knock his tooth out; it was already loose. I just hit him in the mouth with the phone, and his tooth fell out."

That didn't clarify things as much as I think she thought it did. "Oh, I see, but why did you hit him?" She took a deep breath and angrily began to tell me the story.

"Darryl took me to Rome to propose, and last night at dinner instead of proposing, he told me he had changed his mind," she said. "He said 'I've been thinking and I think we should continue to date. I don't think I'm really ready to break it off with my wife. She'll probably try to get half of my million dollar business, and I've worked too hard and long to lose it. Let's just continue to date.'"

Judging by how she spoke and seemed uncoordinated, I suspected that she might have tried to drown her grief in alcohol.

I could understand how disappointed she was and thought the guy had to be a real jerk to get her expectations up and then say that he wasn't going to marry her after all. I said, "Believe me, I sympathize with you and know how angry you are, but this is not the time or place." I lowered my voice so that nobody else could hear us. "Wait until we land in New York and then kick his ass. Just calm down, we have only four more hours."

I thought that would calm her down, but, instead, it seemed to make her angrier and, even more alarmingly, angry at me personally.

She glared at me with an expression that made me hope my teeth would all stay intact. "I don't want to calm down. I want the captain to land this plane now. I want to get off this plane, NOW." She took a deep breath and continued yelling. "I'm exercising my rights. I know we are at a certain longitude and latitude so I'm within my rights to demand to get off."

Now, in all my years of flying, I had never dealt with that particular demand, probably because there's no ruling that says that passengers have a right to demand an unscheduled landing to get off. I was kind of tempted to grant her request to deplane immediately, since we were currently over 10,000 feet over the Atlantic Ocean, but sadly there's also no ruling that allows flight attendants to treat passengers to their own special water landing. Instead, I just told her that I would inform the cockpit crew of her demand and let them know that she was being a disruptive passenger.

One of the other flight attendants called from the cabin telephone system to inform the captain about what I was dealing with. The captain said that the second officer was just about to end his break, and, before returning to the cockpit, he would come to address her issues.

Before he could get to her, she got up, went to the bathroom, locked the door, and started yelling at the very top of her voice that she wanted us to land the plane now.

I knocked on the door and insisted that she quiet down, but she kept on yelling with the door locked. When it was clear that we were not going to get through to her, we manually forced the door open, assisted her out of the bathroom, and walked her to her seat.

Once we got her in her seat, the second officer came up to her. He explained that her disruptive behavior was going to have to stop; there was no way we were going to make an unscheduled stop.

That wasn't good enough for her once she realized he wasn't the captain. She looked at him and said, "I don't want to talk to you. I want the captain."

It's astonishing to look back at all of this after 9/11, because since then, any disruptive passenger is treated as a serious terrorist threat. However, that was then, and when the second officer could see he wasn't getting anywhere with this out of control passenger and returned to the cockpit to ask the captain to come out.

Captain Jackson emerged in full uniform and introduced himself. She repeated her demand that he land the plane now because she wanted to get off. He answered her seriously. "Ms, I'm in charge of this aircraft and our final destination is New York. I don't think you would want me to make an unscheduled stop so you can deplane. I can guarantee you don't want to go to jail in a foreign country, because you would be in jail for a very long time."

She repeated, "I don't care. I just want you to land this plane now." Next, she stood up and unexpectedly changed the subject. "Just how tall are you, anyway?" She wasn't in much of a condition to stand up and immediately stumbled forward onto him.

This was the last straw for the captain. and he finally lost his patience. He looked at me and said, "I want her restrained for the rest of the flight."

I stayed where I was and asked one of the other flight attendants to get the onboard set of handcuffs. Half of the audience in business class was amused by this real-life drama, which was just as tacky as a lot of reality television, plus it had the advantage of being totally unscripted. Others, however, were annoyed that they had paid for and expected a comfortable, relaxed flight with lots of pampering, not a cheap drama from a seemingly drunk passenger. They didn't know that she was going to add yet more drama, including some of the most stereotypical catfight behavior.

The captain and another flight attendant grabbed her hands, and I reached over, ready to snap one of the handcuffs over her wrist. I felt a sudden sharp pain on my forearm, looked down, and saw that she was biting me. She was trying to get her teeth in as deeply as she could, and so I pushed her head back, trying to get her to release her grip. She responded by yanking on my arm so hard that I suffered a whiplash injury to my neck. At the time, though, I didn't even realize the extent of this injury; I was still focused on getting the handcuffs on her.

I moved to approach her from the front, hoping for a better angle that way, and she twisted like a stubborn three-year-old in a tantrum and slid right onto the floor. Her back was against the fuselage, that thin wall, and I ended up straddling her to be able to reach her hands. I guess no matter how old you get, those tomboy fighting tactics always come back to you when you need them. In the struggle, my dress got pushed up, so I was giving everybody who was watching (and everybody was watching) a good view of all my private parts.

Just to make things even less professional-looking, my buttons had gotten unbuttoned, my hair looked like I had been in a windstorm, and my 36Ds were waving in the wind. I was busy trying to get her hands secured and get her off the floor, not paying much attention to the captain's struggle to secure her feet, since just like that toddler in a tantrum, she was kicking and screaming.

Unlike most toddlers, though, she was wearing high-heeled boots, and I saw the captain's face and ears turn bright, bright red. He later explained that she had gotten him right in the most personal and painful parts. It only made him feel a little bit better to know that I had inadvertently punched her right in the breast just a moment earlier. (Why, yes, they did feel like they were mostly artificial.)

We finally got her handcuffed and back in her seat with her seatbelt fastened, but that didn't subdue her at all. She was still screaming her demand for the plane to stop and let her out. Believe me; we were very, very tempted.

Trying to recapture my dignity, I pulled my dress down and ran my fingers through my disheveled hair to regain some order. In the meantime, the captain had been looking on the floor, between the seats and the surrounding area for his glasses; somehow when they had been knocked off his face, they had gotten tangled in my hair during the struggle.

We had already paged a medical doctor and were lucky enough that a psychiatrist was on the flight and came forward to offer her assistance. The four of us eyed the passenger warily. The captain said in a low tone so only the four of us could hear him, "She can't continue like this. It's upsetting all the other passengers." Equally quietly, the psychiatrist suggested that we sedate her, if there was something safe on board.

Whether it was his own idea or whether he was able to overhear us, a passenger called out, "I have some Ativan!" Another yelled, "I have some Librium!" and yet another called out, "I have Xanax." People were rattling the pills in their bottles to get our attention. It felt like we were on board a flying Walgreen's pharmacy or perhaps some kind of reverse auction, with passengers shouting out their offers.

At what were apparently familiar names, the irate passenger suddenly became much more coherent and made her request from among the offerings. The doctor determined that it would be safe to give them to her and got her formal approval to administer the drugs. She finally fell asleep and we were able to continue with our duties and serving other passengers.

Her boyfriend called me over just after she fell asleep. "How is she doing?"

"We finally got her to go to sleep. Everything has finally settled down," I said, still sighing in relief.

He nervously looked at me and said, "Oh, that's good, I've decided that I don't want to press charges when we land in New York. Let's just forget the whole situation."

I could not believe my ears. He wanted us to forget all about her violent outburst and attacks on the flight crew. I sat on the armrest of his seat and let my annoyance and exhaustion show, just a little, as I said, "Sir, you should have controlled this situation about four hours ago. It's too late; we have already called the authorities to meet the flight, and Delta will be pressing charges. Just in case you didn't know, it is a federal offense to harm or interfere with a crew member's duties. I think your girlfriend has committed both offenses."

Once we landed and the front door of the aircraft was opened, the jetway was filled with FBI, NYC police, airport police, Delta agents, management, and my supervisor. (No partridge in a pear tree, though.) The once irate but now sedated passenger was escorted off the aircraft first and placed in a wheelchair. She was arrested and held in jail for several days.

When she came to trial, she was charged with interference of crewmembers' duties and was fined but not sentenced to any jail time. I was told that she had received counseling prior to the hearing and had been diagnosed with bipolar disorder. The court thought that this condition mitigated the circumstances but ordered that she continue with counseling to learn how to control her anger without resorting to violence. The case was considered resolved and closed.

My back pain continued and when I went to the doctor, I found out later that I had a herniated disk in my neck and extensive injuries in my lower back. While the bite marks cleared up fairly soon, my back and neck are still troublesome.

THAT EPISODE HAD ITS FUNNY MOMENTS, but there were also some terrible moments where we couldn't get together afterward and laugh it off. We were in Houston, still boarding last passengers on a flight. Wanda Wilson was working in the first class cabin performing her pre-takeoff beverage service when she asked the gentlemen in row 3A if he would like something to drink. At another glance, she saw that he was very pale and sweating profusely. Wanda asked if he was okay. He looked at her vacantly, seeming unable to answer or perhaps unaware that she had asked him a question.

Wanda immediately called on the aircraft interphone system to Elaine, the flight attendant who was working back in coach with me. She said that a passenger in first class was very sick and would Elaine come and help her. As she headed to the front cabin, Elaine told me what was happening and asked me to go with her.

A sick passenger takes priority over anything else. While it's not common, I wasn't especially alarmed then, mostly because we were still at the gate and could get him medical help immediately. It was the mid-air emergencies that all of us dreaded, especially if we were on an international flight and over the ocean, where we couldn't even make an emergency landing. We always carried emergency medical supplies and medical equipment such as defibrillators, but no flight could ever carry enough to cover all contingencies.

I got to the man first and crouched next to him. I gently rubbed his hand to get his attention and to reassure him that he was with people who were going to help. "Sir, are you okay?" This was our first response question.

He didn't respond. I thought that perhaps asking more loudly, I would get a response. With luck, he'd be able to say what was wrong. I grabbed his shoulder and shook him lightly, repeating more loudly, "Sir, are you okay?" We called this escalation "shake and shout," and it was familiar from our hours upon hours of first aid training.

The next step was to check for a pulse. I was able to feel one, but it was very faint. I loosened his tie and as his head moved to the side, he let out a loud sound that sounded like a snore. I took his pulse again, detecting a very weak pulse, so I decided it best to try to get him on the floor to prepare to perform cardiopulmonary resuscitation (CPR).

While I was doing this, Elaine or Wanda called for assistance. A paramedic and a nurse were on the flight, sitting back in coach. They came forward in response to the emergency call. By the time they arrived, they couldn't find a pulse so they started CPR.

A few minutes later, the airport medical team arrived. Each airport has a team on standby, sometimes right on the premises, other times just a few minutes away. The paramedics continued to work on him for an hour, simultaneously giving him IV (intravenous) saline to keep him hydrated. Then they decided that it was best to try to move him off the airplane to the gurney that was waiting in the jetway. They asked me to come with them and hold the IV bag above my head so that the liquid would continue to flow; the gurney didn't have the holders that they all do today.

The medics continued to work on him, and I asked very quietly, "Do you think he's going to make it?" Without missing a beat or pausing their duties for an instant, one of them responded, "No, I don't think he's going to make it."

Just then, he looked up and saw my eyes fill up with tears. He realized the harsh reality of this man dying was too much for me. He then retreated, "Well, ah ... you never know. He may have a chance. We're going to do our best." I knew that he was trying to make me feel better, but just the fact that he noticed how upset I was helped.

Two baggage handlers, who had been loading the baggage, then came up to see what was going on and if there was anything that we needed them to do. From where they were standing, they couldn't see his face, but I heard one of them say, "I can't see his face, but those look like Joe's boots." He looked at me and then asked, "Excuse me, but do you know this person's name?" Nobody had a chance to look it up or get his ticket to look, so I just said that I didn't know and moved aside so they could see his face.

Their faces immediately filled with shock and grief. He had been a baggage handling instructor and had trained them. Seeing their sense of loss hit me even harder. Passengers are never entirely anonymous to us the way that a stranger on the street is, because the passengers are our responsibility and in our care while they're flying. But encountering somebody who actually knows and mourns for a loss makes it even more personal.

Once he was taken care of, I got back on the plane, we resumed our duties, and took off. When I was next in the airport, I asked if anybody knew what had happened to him. It turned out that he was gravely ill from the moment he was on the aircraft. He had suffered a massive heart attack, and there was really nothing that could have been done for him. At least, he probably never knew what hit him.

I also later found out that the snoring, gurgling sound I had heard when his head moved was the "death rattle," the sound of saliva accumulating in the throat as the body stops swallowing. This shook me as well, since it's the kind of thing a person reads about or hears somebody mention but doesn't expect to hear themselves, unless they are in healthcare.

∞

WE HAD OUR DEFINITE TRIALS AND MOMENTS OF FEAR during flights and at the airport, but we also faced trouble at hotels, where we were especially vulnerable if we didn't know the language or the layout. I was in one very frightening hotel fire and was astonished at how helpless I felt.

In Nice, France, we had a layover at the Harrington Hotel, located on the main drive across from the French Riviera. In America, almost all beaches are made of brownish sand, while on the Riviera, they were comprised of small dark rocks. I can't say that I was paying all that much attention to this interesting geological feature. Several sections of the beach were reserved for nude bathing; I paid proper attention to some of the handsome bodies on full display.

Later that evening, several of us were downstairs with the captain and co-pilot having a few nightcaps. Around midnight, we decided to go up to our rooms, and as we were waiting for the elevator, a large group of people from a tour group was checking in. As I got settled in my bed about thirty minutes later, I heard voices and bumps from the hallway. My first thought was that it was the tour group all finding their rooms at once, but my second thought was that I'd better get up and check it out.

I looked through the peephole to see if I could see anyone. To my amazement, all I saw was a dark hallway, except for the very faint emergency lights. They were faint but I could still see black particles in the air, drifting past the peephole. From our emergency fire training, I knew to check the door with the back of my hand to see if it was hot, which would mean that there was a fire in the hallway. It wasn't, so I slowly opened the door but realized immediately that hallway was too full of smoke to be a safe escape route.

I closed the door and gathered my thoughts, intent on a safe exit. I filled the tub with water and dunked some towels in it, since wet cloth works as a makeshift smoke mask to filter out at least the biggest particles of smoke. I went to the balcony and saw a man on the balcony next door. I asked him what was happening, and while I recognized that he was speaking French, I couldn't make out a single world. But to my great relief, I didn't have to become fluent in five seconds as there was a fire truck with an extended ladder, busy rescuing people about six doors down.

When he saw that I didn't understand him, the man said in broken but comprehensible English that the firemen said we should wait in our rooms for them to come for us. I went back in my room to make sure that the firemen would have a clear pathway if they needed to come into the room, pushing chairs and my luggage out of the way. Since I had to stay there, I also gathered a few necessities (my Delta ID and uniform coat). I hesitated for a moment between my expensive two-piece leather suit and my Delta uniform and figured that it'd be easier to replace the uniform. I returned to the balcony for the fresher air there and to see the progress of the fire fighters. A few moments later, I felt another presence in the room.

I turned around, looking back into the room, and saw a figure straight out of a nightmare. A tall person in bulky clothing, wearing an oversized helmet and a large tank of something on his back, stood there rasping at me. It took a moment to realize that this was a fireman in his firefighting gear, and the mysterious tank was oxygen. I started to walk toward him, but he gestured not to come and said, "Stay, stay, I come back." That left me confused, but I figured he knew what he was doing and it was also what the man on the balcony had said.

By this time, I was much calmer. I knew that the firefighters were there, and they knew that I was in my room, waiting for rescue. I also didn't see flames anywhere. Our position on the third floor also reassured me, since I knew that if worst came to worst, I could tie sheets together and make a rope (which always worked in the movies) to let myself down, or in case not everything that the movies say work actually does work, jump without very serious injury. Like almost everybody, the idea of dying from the actual flames terrified me the most and that simply didn't seem likely. This isn't to say that I wasn't praying, asking God to save us and that if I did have to die like this, let it be quick.

The thought passed through my head that I had just qualified as an interior designer and that if I'd known that my life was destined to end in a French hotel across from a nude beach, I would have studied something other than design, perhaps the nude art on display not far away.

The Frenchman on the balcony called back to me, saying that they still wanted us to stay in our rooms and that they would come for us. They did exactly that in just a few minutes and walked us down the stairs, which were filled with debris and water.

As the on-board leader for the team, I was responsible for making sure that my crew was okay, reporting any injuries to Delta, and for coordinating communications between Delta and the crew. I saw my B line (my assistant and second in command) in an ambulance being given oxygen and went over to find out how she was. She had also been on the third floor but in the wing where the fire had originated. She had severe damage from smoke inhalation, we found, and she was off work for about six months. I suffered less damage and had to take a few months off. (This is longer than an office worker might have to take off because, as flight attendants, we have to have full lung capacity for working up in thinner air and to be ready for physical demands in case of emergencies.)

When I was finally home and didn't have to think about coordinating anything, making sure that my crew was all right, and getting my luggage back (everything smelled like smoke but both my Delta uniform and my leather pantsuit were in fine condition, thanks for asking), that was when I processed the fact that I had been in a fire, that a friend and colleague was seriously hurt, and that it could have been so much more serious than it was. In fact, when I saw my doctor to get checked over and treated for smoke inhalation, he mentioned during our conversation that fire was one of the most agonizing ways to die. It took me some time to process all this and to realize that while it could have been worse, we had all made it out relatively unhurt.

CHAPTER FOURTEEN:

Still We Rise

WHILE THE ATMOSPHERE FOR BLACK FLIGHT ATTENDANTS had changed greatly from the 1970s, we found that sometimes hostility hadn't gone away. It had just gone undercover, and it didn't take much to make it surface. On a flight where a black woman, Cynthia Gathings, was the head flight attendant, another flight attendant informed her that a passenger appeared to have had too much to drink and, as a precaution, had to be cut off from further service. This was the head flight attendant's responsibility. When Cynthia told the passenger, he belligerently called her a "nigger black bitch."

Other passengers and the flight attendants gasped, and one of the flight attendants went to report this to the captain. He asked Cynthia to report her version of the story, which she did. In response, he said only that he didn't want this to turn into an "international incident." That made it clear to Cynthia that he had no intention of taking the appropriate steps to back her up, report the incident, or protect her from this aggressive passenger. In other words, she should just accept being a "nigger black bitch."

Once they landed in London, Cynthia told the story to a female agent, who took it upon herself to have the passenger escorted off the plane. No passenger, she said, was going to talk to any crew member in that way. I wish I could say that this took place in earlier days, but this happened in late 1998.

∽o∾

THAT SAID, WE MADE GREAT STRIDES, so let's take a moment to celebrate them. The first black pilot was probably Ahmet Ali Çelikten, a Turk of African descent, who was a military pilot in World War I. Eugene Jacques Bullard (born Eugene James Bullard) was almost certainly the second black pilot and was definitely the first African American one. However, he immigrated to France as a young man, and during World War I, he flew for the French military, as part of the legendary Foreign Legion (as a foreigner, he was unable to join the French main military). Ironically, when the United States entered the war, it recruited Americans who had joined the French military, but because Bullard was black, he was considered ineligible, despite his having participated in roughly twenty combat missions.

The first black female commercial pilot in the United States was Janet Harmon Waterford Bragg, whom you'll remember from the opening and the history of the Coffey School.

In 1992 we and the rest of America were thrilled by another pioneer, Dr. Mae Jemison, who also grew up in Chicago (another tie back to the city). As a young girl, she figured that space travel would be routine by the time that she grew up, but to make sure it happened, she insisted on a career in the sciences. She entered Stanford at age sixteen, graduating with a Bachelor of Science in Chemical Engineering and enough credits to have also earned a Bachelor of Arts in African and Afro-American Studies. She went to Cornell and earned her medical degree.

In 1983 Sallie Ride, the first American woman in space, and Nichelle Nichols, from Robbins, Illinois, who portrayed Lieutenant Uhura on *Star Trek*, inspired her to apply for NASA, and she was admitted in 1987. (She later appeared as a guest star on *Star Trek: The Next Generation* in 1993.) Jemison went into space on the shuttle Endeavor from September 12–20, 1992. She's also written several books about her life and is a very popular speaker.

Ten years after Jemison's flight, Captain Vernice Armour, also from Chicago, was the first female African American Marine Corps naval aviator and also their first African American female combat pilot. Both her parents were military members, as was one of her grandfathers, and she enlisted in the army reserve and later joined the ROTC. Her childhood dream, though, was to be a mounted police officer, and in 1996, she joined the Nashville police and became the first African American woman on their motorcycle squad. (It wasn't a horse but pretty close.)

During an ROTC career day, she saw a black woman's image in a pilot's suit and was immediately inspired to become a pilot herself. Two years later, she joined the marines and became their first black female pilot. In March 2003, she flew an attack helicopter in the US invasion of Iraq and thus became the Marine Corps' first black female combat pilot. Her missions were based from Kuwait, and often she would return to the base there with bullets in the helicopter. She returned to Iraq for two further tours of duty and added the Iraq Campaign Medal, with two service stars, to her already impressive list of military honors.

Back in the States, she served as a diversity officer and liaison to the Pentagon. She is also a pioneer as an open lesbian military member, and her first major publication was an essay in the Marine Corps University Press's book, *Th End of Don't Ask Don't Tell.*

She left the marines in 2007 and in 2011 wrote her book, *Zero to Breakthrough: The 7-Step, Battle-Tested Method for Accomplishing Goals that Matter* in which she tells her story and describes the process that she used, which she calls the Zero to Breakthrough™ Success Plan. Like so many of our pioneers in the sky, something in her heart and mind never stopped flying, and she says that she often refers to "plans of attack" and "flight plans" when talking about goals and strategies.

One of the first commercial flights with an all-female African American crew was on February 12, 2009, on Atlantic Southeast Airlines (a subsidiary of Sky West), flying from Atlanta to Nashville on a CRJ700. The crew included Captain Rachelle Jones, First Officer Stephanie Grant (no relation), and flight attendants Diana Galloway and Robin Rogers. This historic event took place during Black History Month.

Although Mae Jamison was the first African American to enter the space program, long before her mission were a few black woman, unknown to most Americans. They were behind the desks at NASA, manually calculating the trajectory for Alan Shepard in 1961, the first American in space, and later for John Glenn, who personally requested that Katherine Johnson, the human computer as she was known, personally check the electronic calculations before his flight aboard Friendship 7 in 1962.

On November 24, 2015, Ms. Johnson received the nation's highest civilian award, the Presidential Medal of Freedom, from President Barack H. Obama, and in Century Fox will release the movie, *Hidden Figures,* telling the hese mathematicians: Katherine G. Johnson, Dorothy Monaé, the brains behind one of the greatest

❦

SINCE OUR EARLY DAYS AS STARS IN THE SKIES, many things have changed, making flying less glamorous and exciting for all involved. Airlines have vanished, and new ones are struggling. The major airlines have consolidated to survive the mergers that have become far too common.

The airlines have changed dramatically as well as the composition of the passengers. Flight attendant uniforms are more for comfort and for ease of movement than for glamour; you rarely see sky-high heels anymore. To Delta's credit, the company maintains its professional image by conducting uniform checks, and customers in a recent survey voted Delta's red uniform the most popular of all their uniform combinations.

Because the economy has gone through such demise and devastation, customer service has been redefined and revised to survive. Airlines used to offer deluxe services to all customers, starting with short lines at check-in and personable skycaps to greet you with a warm welcome. Some skycaps grew to recognize frequent flyers and would ask about a flier's last trip and would even provide advice on various destinations such as the best restaurants or hotels. They were true ambassadors for the airlines and set the tone for a wonderful flying experience. Now, time pressures don't allow them or flyers that kind of luxury any more.

Many airlines have been driven to find the newest way to extract more money from their customers, including charging for things that used to be free like blankets, magazines, meals, or pillows. Seats are becoming narrower and so is the space between rows. The lack of space between the rows and reclining seats reducing the amount of space behind them has driven passengers to fight, and some pilots have even been forced to divert flights to get the combatants off the plane. The latest product offered by Delta on all two-cabin aircraft in their entire fleet is Delta Comfort, which provides customers with more pitch (similar to seats in the exit row) and access to priority boarding. Delta Comfort seats are located in the first few rows of the main cabin.

Getting to one's destination used to be half the fun, but today many people consider flying a necessary inconvenience, due to the added screening process and other check-in requirements. On top of all that, the travel industry is in constant jeopardy from either manmade disasters such as another travel-related terrorist attack, or natural ones, such as pandemic disease.

In 2009, during the H1N1 pandemic, the World Health Organization considered only travel restrictions, but so many travelers, especially in Asia, canceled travel plans that it was a major slowdown for the industry. In today's world with so many travelers and so many locations accessible by air, governments, health agencies, and travel organizations are deeply concerned about the potential spread of highly communicable diseases like Middle East Respiratory Syndrome (MERS) and Ebola with caution, since air travel could become a vector for a local outbreak of a disease to become global. In the past, diseases such as bubonic plague and influenza turned out to be global killers because of newly-opened travel routes or a sudden number of infected travelers, and this could happen again, only perhaps even faster.

By 2000, many airlines, including Delta, were already in financial trouble, and pay and benefits were declining. Of course, 9/11 accelerated this. Ongoing fears of terrorism and the hassles of increased security made flying an even more tense experience for crews alike. Airlines were trying to pack planes even more tightly than ever, and most flights were entirely full or overbooked, which meant bumping people off flights. As much as I loved travel, it was starting to become a burden, as was my commute from Chicago to New York, which was then my base.

Bad days on the job seemed more and more frequent, with frayed nerves everywhere. Finally, one particularly chaotic flight had reconfirmed that our days of being regarded as glamorous, almost movie star status, were over. We were no longer the coiffed young "stewardesses" admired by men and women, the "crème la crème," the center of men and women's fantasies and dreams. The days when the make up was always impeccable, nails manicured, high heels polished and in stellar condition, being the most desirable weight and size, and our uniforms exemplified our attributes were gone. Then uniforms usually had been designed by a well-known designer and were altered to perfection. And we projected the look of innocence to be cherished and protected by all.

Delta started offering retirement incentives, and by 2005, I was ready to start a new phase in my life, as were many of the pioneers I had worked with from the start. I finished my interior design degree and was anxious to use it. Finally, one of the retirement packages seemed like an offer that I didn't want to refuse, and so I set down my wings.

∽o∾

TO SUPPLEMENT MY INCOME, I created my own interior design company, ECG Design Interiors. I do residential interior design and staging for home sales with a co-worker friend, Kai Behnke, setting up the interiors to look as enticing as possible to potential owners but still neutral enough that they can see themselves there.

Others took up different careers or supplemental part-time jobs. Patricia Grace Murphy is involved in community service in Florida, Eugene Harmond is still flying and started an art gallery part-time, specializing in African art, much of which he bought on his trips. Elaine McKinney became a nurse, and Phenola Culbreath-Smith became a real estate agent. Terry Taylor and Gerri Walker are both deeply engaged in community service, as is Debra Surrett as the First Lady of Calvary Community Church in South Holland, IL. Cynthia Gathings and Dot Daniels began their second career in the school system. Wanda Wilson currently works toward her master's degree at divinity school in California. Sarah Qualls is a bus driver and dispatcher for a children's bus service in Illinois—looks like the travel bug definitely didn't leave her. Almost any career that you can name, there's probably a retired flight attendant doing it. Others are simply enjoying retirement, including, in many cases, the joys of being grandparents.

Some beloved colleagues didn't make it to retirement. Aside from the untimely deaths of the two Brenda's, we lost several of our early male colleagues to AIDS during the 1980s.

The camaraderie that we developed during those early days has stood the test of time. We have been there for each other through marriages, childbirths, deaths of loved ones and peers, divorces, and illness. We try to get together from time to time. One event I look forward to attending is an elegant New Year's Eve brunch given by the Sky Girls, a private group of retired Delta flight attendants in Houston. The brunch is hosted by Angele Creuzot and Margaret Flint, and the menu ranges from caviar and a signature cocktail to live entertainment and a five-course meal delivered by servers. It is a wonderful way to start off the New Year, or end the year with a summer event hosted by Phyllis Calvin and experience the same elegant treatment and exquisite menu.

In many ways, we're just as close as we were when we started our careers, through all the changes and frequent chaos, both good and bad. I can't imagine any other career that has the same kind of excitement, challenges, and rewards.

To all the future flight attendant ladies and gentlemen out there, best wishes, and when you reach the stars, give a thought to all of us and know that your blessings are as numerous as the *Stars in the Sky.*

"If there's a book that you want to read,
but it hasn't been written yet,
then you must write it."
Toni Morrison

CPSIA information can be obtained
at www.ICGtesting.com
Printed in the USA
BVOW08s0808220217
476861BV00001B/51/P